MW01076726

# TESTIMONIALS

I met Gerry Valentine many years ago when we worked together at Pfizer Pharmaceuticals. I was always impressed with the integrity of his leadership style, so I was delighted when he launched his executive coaching business. I knew he would bring that same integrity to his clients. I was even more delighted when he published a book, *The Thriving Mindset—Tools for Empowerment in a Disruptive World*, because it was the next step in delivering that integrity, and at a time when we need it more than ever. Two important values I live by in my own life are "be your authentic self in every aspect of your life" and "to whom much is given, much will be required." Gerry exemplifies those values in his book. By sharing authentic stories from his personal and professional journey—both the triumphs and the setbacks—Gerry provides an essential guide for anyone looking to overcome disruption and challenges (things we will all face), or allowing them to find, as Gerry puts it, the "advantage that is often just on the other side of the adversity."

— *Vivian Armstrong, Vice President and Head of Corporate Technology, New York Life Insurance Company*

"Authenticity and empowerment from within are central to every lesson Gerry Valentine teaches, especially in *The Thriving Mindse—Tools for Empowerment in a Disruptive World,*

Through a wide array of easily digestible narratives and studies, Mr. Valentine has crafted an essential guide that can help everyone, from startup to C-Suite, leverage lessons learned from disruption to achieve new success."

— *Jonathan Lovitz, Business & Public Policy Advocate; Senior Vice President, National LGBT Chamber of Commerce (NGLCC)*

I am Odell Mays, Principal and Founder of Mays2 Consulting, a specialized practice working with nonprofits on organizational sustainability issues. I am also an adjunct faculty at Columbia University. Gerry and I met in 1986 at NYU Graduate School of Business, and we have remained close friends and confidantes ever since. Gerry has an amazing, prescient ability to make connections between "life events" and "life actions." His clear-headed, and analytical mindset really defines the concept of thriving, and he shares that mindset in a most generous way.

I have had the privilege of watching Gerry embrace and embody the ideas set forth in this well-written, accessible, practical book. More than ever, we need authors and speakers who can help us make sense and make a plan for thriving during these disruptive and difficult times. This book is a must-read!

— *Odell Mays II, Principal and Founder, Mays2 Consulting*

When I first met Gerry nearly 20 years ago, I was a consultant, and he was a client. I was immediately struck by his thoughtfulness and equanimity under pressure. A few years later, I ended up leading that same organization and promoted him.

He quickly proved to be the most natural manager I ever saw, guiding his reports to improved performance. When he became an executive coach, I naturally started referring clients to him. Not surprisingly, they described him as a lifesaver. Should you read this book? Obviously, my answer is yes.

— *Tony Fross, Partner and Co-lead Organization & Culture Practice, Prophet*

"In **The Thriving Mindset**, thought-leader Gerry Valentine connects the dots on how our pace of change is disrupting the calm in our society, inciting fear and radicalized behavior. If we don't learn to embrace change, we have a very dangerous chance of being left behind in a rapidly evolving landscape. Gerry's just the dot-connector our country needs to help us navigate through these tumultuous times. I will be recommending this book to many."

— *Tamara Palmer, Founder Greyzone and published Fiction Writer*

Gerry Valentine's book, **The Thriving Mindset—Tools for Empowerment in a Disruptive World**, is an essential guide for anyone looking to make positive change in the world. As a Partner at LIFT Economy, a company that is dedicated to creating an inclusive economy that works for the benefit of all life, I know how demanding true change-making can be. It takes courage and insight, the ability to see beyond knee-jerk urgencies of the moment, and the ability to take on the bigger issues in the world around us. Those demands are more daunting than ever before, as we face a global pandemic, ever-increasing economic inequality, a long-overdue reckoning with racial injustice, the climate crisis, and more. This book provides invaluable tools for people who want to make a positive difference in the world—tools to tap into their best selves, to lead in authentic and value-based ways, and to inspire the best in others.

*— Ryan Honeyman, Partner at LIFT Economy,*
*Co-Founder at Force for Good Fund,*
*Co-Author of "The B Corp Handbook"*

*The Thriving Mindset—Tools for Empowerment in a Disruptive World* zooms out to look at the big picture of why and how to turn adversity into advantage, as it also provides a close, in-depth, highly practical guide to addressing these challenges. Valentine highlights how the work of disruptive, empowered leadership is continuous, requiring an honest consideration of one's own strengths and areas of improvement in order to seize the opportunity and support growing teams and companies. Gerry Valentine is a renowned TEDx speaker, global business advisor, and executive leadership coach, with deep expertise in the Fortune 500 and technology sectors impacted by a disruption. The thoughtful management practices Valentine shares ripple outwards to improve teams, companies, and communities. This book is a highly valuable resource for anyone interested in becoming an empowered disruptor and thriving during adversity.

*— Sarah E. Brown, Head of Marketing at Intricately,*
*Founder and Co-Organizer at Flatirons Tech*

I met Gerry Valentine many years ago when we worked together at Pfizer, Inc. Since then, I've watched and admired how he has nurtured and grown his executive coaching practice, no doubt due to the attention he pays to others. I was especially delighted to see him publish this book. I believe that we rise by lifting others, and lifting others is precisely what Gerry accomplishes in this book. Through examining his own life-path and career—generously sharing triumphs and setbacks—Gerry allows us to benefit from his vast experience. He's delivering this message at a critical time. Right now, many people are facing disruption and/or uncertainty in their careers and in many other parts of life. I know from my own career that, even in the best of times, we all need support and guidance on how to overcome the challenges that naturally emerge along the way. *The Thriving Mindset* provides just that.

*— Niesha N. Foster, Vice President, Global Health & Patient Access, Pfizer Inc.*

We are facing an unprecedented time, and business leaders are playing a critical role in finding the solutions our society needs. As the founder and CEO of Out Leadership, that's something I know first-hand. At Out Leadership, we help global companies innovate, transform, and reap the business benefits of inclusion—we call it *"Return on Equality."* That means tapping into the immense talent the LGBTQ+ community can bring to organizations, especially at the senior leadership level—talent that helps companies transform and innovate at critical moments. That's exactly what Gerry Valentine epitomizes in this book. Drawing on his own background as both a Fortune 100 leader and a person belonging to multiple underrepresented groups—a gay man, an African American man, and a person who grew up in poverty—Valentine taps into those experiences as a source of insight, innovation, and inspiration. This book is an excellent guide for all of us as we navigate what lies ahead.

*— Todd Sears, Founder and CEO, Out Leadership*

I met Gerry when we were colleagues at Pfizer. I was in Commercial Operations, and Gerry was my Business Technology partner. For the team I was on to be successful, we needed to be able to partner with Gerry's organization. Gerry spent a tremendous amount of time redirecting discussions and activities towards common goals and what could be accomplished; in other words, he helped us identify our opportunities. As a result, we were able to make progress. The mindset of identifying opportunities in the face of challenges or things we do not understand is essential, and a book like this is the key. The world needs positivity.

*— Debbie Reynolds, Vice President,*
*Analytic Tools and Platforms at Pfizer Inc.*

"I was incredibly inspired while looking through the manuscript, and as a small business owner and homeschooling parent, I am definitely part of the audience demographic. The timing for this book is perfect, with the entire world reeling from the disruption of COVID-19. Mr. Valentine's book will help people in leadership roles make important cognitive shifts necessary to be successful during this turbulent period."

*— Gail Marlene Schwartz, Founder, Gail Writes*
*Copywriting and Editing*

# THE
# THRIVING
# MINDSET

# THE
# THRIVING
# MINDSET

Tools for Empowerment
in a Disruptive World

## GERRY VALENTINE

PUBLISH
YOUR
PURPOSE
PRESS

Publish Your Purpose Press
141 Weston Street, #155
Hartford, CT, 06141

PUBLISH YOUR PURPOSE PRESS

The opinions expressed by the Author are not necessarily those held by Publish Your Purpose Press.

Ordering Information: Quantity sales and special discounts are available on quantity purchases by corporations, associations, and others. For details, contact the publisher at orders@publishyourpurposepress.com.

Edited by: Hunter Liguore and Emily Austin
Cover design by: Nelly Murariu of PixBee Design
Typeset by: Medlar Publishing Solutions Pvt Ltd., India

Printed in the United States of America.
ISBN: 978-1-951591-34-2 (paperback)
ISBN: 978-1-951591-35-9 (ebook)

Library of Congress Control Number: 2020920842

First edition, March 2021.

The information contained within this book is strictly for informational purposes. The material may include information, products, or services by third parties. As such, the Author and Publisher do not assume responsibility or liability for any third-party material or opinions. The publisher is not responsible for websites (or their content) that are not owned by the publisher. Readers are advised to do their own due diligence when it comes to making decisions.

The mission of Publish Your Purpose Press is to discover and publish authors who are striving to make a difference in the world. We give marginalized voices power and a stage to share their stories, speak their truth, and impact their communities. Do you have a book idea you would like us to consider publishing? Please visit PublishYourPurposePress.com for more information.

# DEDICATION

*This book is dedicated to my husband, life partner, and soul-mate, Daniel Blausey. Daniel, I love you with all my heart, and I am grateful every day for the amazing journey that is the life we have built together.*

# TABLE OF CONTENTS

# FOREWORD

As an author, speaker, and consultant, I'm always looking to connect with innovators in the field of business. It has long been my goal to empower others to make beneficial changes in their lives and to support self-reinvention. That goal of inspiring positive change is what led me to write my books— *Stand Out*, *Reinventing You*, and *Entrepreneurial You*. It's also what has brought me to meet Gerry Valentine and to recommend his important book, *The Thriving Mindset*.

I first met Gerry at a time in his life when he was working to reinvent himself. He had already completed a long and successful Fortune 100 corporate career, but he believed he had something more to offer the world. Over the years we've known each other, I've seen how his message has emerged— one that's not just about his professional career, but also about who he is, his values and beliefs, and his deeply personal and courageous reflection on his life's journey. In the pages that follow, you'll see that Gerry's path was, in many ways, an extremely unlikely one. But it was also one that yielded critical lessons in how to, as Gerry puts it, "turn life's adversities into advantages." Gerry breaks these lessons down into specific steps and tools that anyone can use to overcome setbacks and thrive in disruptive times.

This book comes at a critical time. Many of us are feeling overwhelmed by disruptive forces coming from many fronts— the COVID-19 pandemic, social and political unrest, and environmental disasters, just to name a few. This book offers a message of hope. Gerry explains how disruption—even the extreme disruption we're facing—also brings opportunity. He provides a guide for how people can learn to navigate past the challenges of the moment and find the opportunities that are inevitably on the other side of the disruption.

There have been times in my own career when I've been faced with obstacles and uncertainty—and I've had to learn to adapt and change my mindset in order to overcome them. Gerry's book, *The Thriving Mindset*, offers real, tangible methods and thought-provoking exercises that will guide readers through even the most overwhelming and uncertain times, and offer them clarity in a world barraged by disruption.

Dorie Clark
*September 2020*
*New York City*

# ACKNOWLEDGEMENTS

This book is the result of an unlikely five-decade life journey that was, in many ways, exceedingly challenging, and one that I feel extremely privileged and grateful to have had. And, of course, a journey that continues to unfold in exciting and unexpected ways. No one achieves anything of substance alone. There have been many people who have helped me over the years, in both big and small ways, and more people than I could possibly hope to thank in these pages; however, I want to mention some of the people who have been exceptionally helpful along the way to writing this book.

First, thank you to my husband, **Daniel Blausey**, for your unwavering support and love as I've grown and explored new directions in life. You amaze and inspire me every day.

Thank you to my best friend, **Odell Mays**, (for thirty-five years and counting) for the warmth and inspiration of our relationship. There have been so many times when I wouldn't have made it through without you; you are simply the best.

Thank you to my dear friend, **Sarah Rebrick**, for your love and support. I'm so glad you're in my life. I always feel so much better (and so much smarter) after I spend time with you.

Thank you to my good friend, **Steve Salee**, for your camaraderie and for our many inspiring conversations. I'm so grateful for your thought-partnership and kind encouragement.

Thank you, **Tony Fross**. You are truly one of the smartest people I've ever known. It was a privilege to work with you. You always inspired my thinking, and I'm grateful to now call you a good friend.

Thank you, **Tami Palmer**, for your encouragement when I began this (very unlikely) process of becoming a writer, and for all the encouragement that has followed since.

Thank you to my aunt, **Gale Surrency**, for showing me the true meaning of grace. You are a role model and an inspiration always.

Thank you to my late mother, **Zipporah Carter**, for everything you did, against so many odds, and through challenges that I can barely imagine. I know I got some of my favorite traits—my strength, tenacity, and resilience—from you.

And thank you to the many clients and organizations I've had the great privilege of working with. You have each made me a little smarter, a little more insightful, and a little more compassionate.

I will always be immensely grateful for each of you.

# LETTER TO THE READER

$D$ear Reader:

I've been thinking about the word *crucible* a lot over the last several months. A crucible is defined as a *"severe test"* or *"a situation in which concentrated forces interact to cause change."*

As I completed writing this book—a book on thriving through disruption—we were in the eleventh month of the COVID-19 pandemic, arguably the most significant disruption in a century. More than 410,000 people in the U.S. have already died from COVID-19—that's more than the number of Americans who died in World War II. By the time you read this letter, the COVID death toll will be higher. But, the disruption caused by COVID is much broader: 30 million Americans—roughly one in five people—have lost their jobs because of COVID; food pantries across the country report surges in hunger—because many people who lost jobs were already living on the edge; economists warn of long-term economic damage and a recovery that may take years. And, at the same time, we're forced to reckon with societal ills that have festered for far too long: racial injustice in the U.S.; police violence against innocent Black and Brown people; climate change that's causing record-breaking wildfires and storms; the continuing impact of economic inequality—just to name a few. This is truly a time when *concentrated forces are interacting to cause change.*

For me, part of the *crucible* has been testing whether the ideas I put forth in this book are equal to the challenges of this moment. When I began writing this book, almost two years ago, I had no idea humanity would be facing disruption at the scale of COVID-19 when the book went to press, and so, this book is not about the pandemic. However, I've also come to believe that the ideas in the following chapters are extremely relevant to the disruption and uncertainty of this moment.

One of the most important principles I put forward is that disruption is always accompanied by opportunity. Some of the greatest achievements are, in fact, the response to some kind of disruption. I hope the tools I provide for cultivating *The Thriving Mindset* will help you find those bright spots of opportunity amid the disruption, no matter what the coming months bring.

Sincerely,
Gerry Valentine

CHAPTER ONE

# UNDERSTANDING
# *THE THRIVING MINDSET*

Why does change, uncertainty, and disruption cause some people to break and others to break records? This is a question I've been drawn to for most of my life—a question that has become more important than ever before.

We're living through one of the most disruptive periods in human history. We're witnessing rapid change that's impacting virtually every aspect of how we live and how we work. It's not just the scale of change, but also the pace of change, that is causing a lot of anxiety, fear, and even pessimism. Entire industries become obsolete virtually overnight, companies struggle to evolve and adapt, and even highly-educated professionals can feel under threat as they struggle to keep pace.

However, there's a different perspective on disruption, one that embraces it as a source of opportunity. People who take this perspective are able to turn the anxiety into excitement. They respond to disruption with hope and innovation, rather than descending into fear and pessimism. And they utilize change and uncertainty as an advantage. They are the ones who often go on to break records.

For almost thirty years, I've worked at some of the world's most prestigious Fortune 100 companies—companies that were not only successful but also faced tremendous upheaval and disruption. I've coached leaders in a broad range of organizations—from scrappy start-ups to global giants—all of which needed to navigate disruption and change. My personal life experience has also required me to negotiate a tremendous amount of disruption and uncertainty. I've learned something important about what it takes to succeed in the face of disruption, and about what sets the people who succeed apart from everyone else. I call it *The Thriving Mindset*.

People who cultivate a *Thriving Mindset* see change, disruption, and uncertainty as a source of opportunity. They prepare themselves so that they are ready to take advantage of opportunity—when the time is right, they seize opportunity. People who cultivate a *Thriving Mindset* suffer setbacks like anyone else, but instead of just surviving, they learn, adapt and grow, and ultimately become better *because* of— not in spite of—whatever disruption they've experienced. That's what allows them to go on to break records, rather than being broken.

This book provides the skills and day-to-day practices needed to develop *The Thriving Mindset*. It is written as a hands-on guide for successfully navigating disruptive change and for finding the opportunities to excel that disruptive change often presents. In the following chapters, you'll find stories and case studies from my own experience; the companies I've worked with, known, or studied; and the many talented individuals I've had the very great privilege to coach and advise. For the sake of confidentiality, I've substituted fictional names and altered any identifiable details to keep the anonymity of those mentioned. Equally, I will share a set of proven assessments, tools, and frameworks I've developed over my career and personal life that will give you the ability to thrive through disruption.

Collectively, if we create more people who, rather than being broken by disruptions, can become the ones to break records, we can create a better world.

## WHY THE THRIVING MINDSET IS CRITICAL

To understand **The Thriving Mindset** and why it's so critical, we first must understand two different perspectives on today's world. From one perspective, we're living in a time of unprecedented opportunity, and there's evidence that many companies have ridden that wave: innovative new enterprises like Zoom, Netflix, Slack, and many others are making their mark, defining entirely new markets, and displacing long-standing incumbents. Technology, remote work, and globalization have made it possible to perform many jobs from anywhere in the world, allowing many people to become free agents—liberated from being shackled to a single employer. Innovative technologies have also created entirely new, in-demand, and well-compensated professions—jobs like big data analyst, social media manager, and SEO specialist didn't exist a decade ago. And because technology continues to erase barriers to entry for start-ups, many people have found there has never been a better time to become an entrepreneur. If you have an idea for the next great widget, you can literally create a website on Squarespace tonight and start selling on Amazon tomorrow. That's how many of today's most successful billionaires started—people like Jeff Bezos, Mark Zuckerberg, and Jack Dorsey.

But many people in the U.S. are facing a very different reality: they are being left out. They are being left behind. They are at the breaking point. They feel overwhelmed by disruption, and they are unable to keep up with the pace of change. Put plainly, they spend most of their time frightened about the future. Every time an innovative start-up disrupts a long-standing industry incumbent, the people who work for that incumbent (typically numbering in the thousands) are also disrupted. The same pace of change and disruption that has led some to innovation, opportunity, and success is taking others to the breaking point.

Here's the big problem we face, both as individuals and as a society: we do a very poor job preparing people for a changing world, especially for the kind of disruptive change we have now. In my executive coaching practice, I frequently meet individuals who are desperately searching for a place where they'll be "safe" from change and disruption. Sometimes, they think safety can be found through a career change or getting in with a particular company. Often, they long for the kinds of careers their parents had, where you could get a job with a "good company," work hard and do the right thing, and expect to move up along a set career path until retirement.

I've seen the same dynamic in organizations. I've worked with many companies (both large and small) that found themselves facing some significant disruptive change in their business. It might have been the entry of a new competitor, the loss of exclusivity on a patent, or a new technology that made their core product obsolete. In many cases, leaders at those organizations desperately try to return to the safety of a past that no longer exists. It's a dangerous pursuit that generally ends in disaster.

My answer to those seeking safety is always the same: *The career expectations our parents had are about a past that will never return. There are no safe companies or careers. The only safety you will find is the safety you create for yourself.*

## UNDERSTANDING TODAY'S PACE OF CHANGE

Ultimately, **The Thriving Mindset** is about understanding the change we see in today's world and preparing for the pace, scope, and complexity of that change.

Here are several key elements I'm witnessing:

- **New technology is emerging quickly and impacting very large numbers of people.** Social media is perhaps the most dramatic example of how this rapid rise is changing social norms. Today, there are approximately 3.5 billion social media users worldwide (Clement, Number of global social network users 2017–2025, 2020); that's 45% of the global population. For the first time in history, almost half of humanity has the ability to instantly connect with one another. The three biggest social media platforms are each enormous—Facebook: 2.5 billion monthly active users (MAUs); YouTube: 1.9 billion MAUs; and WhatsApp: 1.5 billion MAUs (Lua, n.d.). To put these numbers into more perspective, consider this: there are more Facebook users than Christians (Hackett and McClendon, 2017)—and consider that it took Christianity over 2,000 years to reach those numbers. Facebook did it in just 15 years. Together, these new social media platforms, along with other new technologies, have had a dramatic impact on how we live and interact with one another.

- **New technologies have created entirely new (previously unimaginable) companies, and they are decimating long-standing incumbents.** The smartphone is less than 20 years old, but it has enabled companies like Uber, Airbnb, and Amazon to become dominant forces that have disrupted long-standing industries. Airbnb now books more hotel nights than the top five hotel chains (Marriott International, Hilton Worldwide, Intercontinental Hotel Group, Wyndham Worldwide, and Accor Hotel Group) combined (McDermid, Airbnb's number of listings surpasses rooms held by top five hotel brands combined, 2017).

- **The rise of big tech, and the start-ups it has helped build, has caused companies to turn over faster than ever before.** More than 50% of the companies that were on the Fortune 500 list in the year 2000 are no longer there (Bonnet, Buvat, and KVJ, n.d.). That's because they've been replaced with newer companies with more innovative ideas.

- **Advancements in technology have already displaced many low-skilled workers, and there's more displacement to come.** Manufacturing in the United States has been in decline since the 1970s, shrinking from 28 percent of total employment in 1960 to eight percent in 2017 (DeSilver, 2017). There's a popular narrative about manufacturing "repatriation" since 2008, but the true picture is more nuanced. The manufacturing that has returned is highly automated, meaning far more work can be done with far fewer workers. Industrial robots are now burning welds, painting cars, assembling products, handling materials, and packaging and shipping things. This trend toward automation is accelerating. For example, Amazon started exploring the use of robotics in 2012 with the purchase of a young robotics company called Kiva Systems, giving them ownership over a new breed of mobile robots that can move freely around factories by reading barcodes placed on the floor. Today, Amazon has deployed more than 200,000 factory robots (Del Rey, 2019) and credits the devices with improving both speed and efficiency in the company's operations (Amazon Staff, n.d.).

- **Better-educated, higher-paid workers will be the next to be impacted.** A new study by the Brookings Institute (Muro, Winton, and Maxim, 2019) projects that high-skilled professionals like radiologists, legal professionals, optometrists, sales professionals, management analysts, computer programmers, and many others may be the most impacted by new technologies, like Artificial Intelligence (AI). We've already seen signs of this shift. For example, there is already AI technology that is better at identifying cancer on test results than a human radiologist (Grady, 2019). This is a dramatic departure from the prior perspective that only low-skilled workers needed to worry.

- **The future of work will look very different from today.** Some have estimated that up to one-third of the U.S. workforce could be displaced by automation by 2030 (Manyika, Lund, et al., Jobs lost, jobs gained: What the future of work will mean for jobs, skills, and wages, 2017).

In the future, there will be far less manual work, and people will be required to work in tandem with computers. For example, no one currently expects the aforementioned AI technology to completely replace human radiologists, but rather that doctors and other professionals will use these types of technologies to improve productivity. This also means that workers at all levels will need to rapidly learn new technologies in order to keep pace with each successive advancement.

- **People are feeling more pressure.** Companies that have spurred the "gig" economy (companies like Uber, Handy, and Lyft) have moved many people into an unpredictable lower-paying, less secure lifestyle. Recent college grads often struggle to find employment, and many people still have not recovered from the losses of the "Second Great Recession" of 2008/2009. The Baby Boomer generation was especially hard hit by the last recession, and many are finding that they'll need to work to a much later age than they had anticipated (Thompson, 2011). This means that they'll retire *much* later than expected (if they retire at all) and be exposed to even more change and uncertainty through their careers. Moreover, the fact that Baby Boomers are not retiring means that many Generation Xers are finding it harder to progress in their careers because Baby Boomers haven't exited, compounding the impact of the Great Recession on the younger generation (Urban, 2019).

- **We're seeing unanticipated negative consequences from technologies that were supposed to connect us.** In theory, creating the ability for vast portions of humanity to connect with one another offers an incredible opportunity for mutual understanding and collaboration. That was the anticipated benefit of social media platforms like Facebook, Twitter, and others. In reality, social media has also provided a forum for misinformation, hate-speech, and fomenting discontent and social anxiety. Here are just a few examples: social media has been used by foreign government to interfere in national elections; the lack of fact-checking and journalistic integrity (as exists in traditional media) has opened the door for online disinformation campaigns; and social media platforms have become a forum for hate groups and white supremacists to gather followers.

- **It's more than just technology-driven disruption: widespread financial disruptions are also causing tremendous distress.** Technology-driven change is not the only source of anxiety. It's not even the biggest. According to the American Psychological Association (APA), financial stress is the number one cause of anxiety in the United States. At the beginning of 2020, the United States was in the longest economic expansion in history. However, large numbers of people were in financial distress. That's because most of the economic gains were going to the ultra-rich. The middle class was actually shrinking, and poverty rates were on the rise. Some economists estimate that half the American population is living under what is called "financial distress," meaning that they are living paycheck-to-paycheck and have very little (if anything) in savings. Some studies have shown that 40 percent of Americans would struggle to cover an unexpected expense of as little as $400; so, a disruption like a lost job or medical emergency could quickly land them in a desperate situation. (Gabler, 2016). Then came the COVID pandemic which, at the time of this writing, had plunged an additional eight million Americans into poverty. (We'll talk more about personal finances in Chapter 9, Understanding Wealth and Creating Financial Health.)

## WE'VE SEEN THIS BEFORE: HISTORICAL CONTEXT FOR DISRUPTIVE CHANGE

As daunting as the pace of change may feel right now, there is a historical precedent. The industrial revolution that started in the 1700s brought a similar level of widespread disruption. In fact, some have called what we're witnessing a "fourth industrial revolution" (Schwab, n.d.). I believe we can gain insight into what's happening now by examining the prior waves of disruptive change—the three prior industrial revolutions—each of which has important lessons.

The first industrial revolution began in Great Britain in the early 18th century and spread to other parts of the world from there (The Encyclopaedia Britannica, n.d.). It was spurred largely by the invention of the coal-fired steam engine, which led to the automation of factories and a shift from manual production processes to machine-powered manufacturing. The second industrial revolution happened in the late 19th and early 20th centuries (The Encyclopaedia Britannica, n.d.). It was characterized by a growth in global technology, like the introduction of mass electrification, the electric motor, the incandescent lightbulb, and electric communication like the telegraph. The second industrial revolution also included rapid expansion of many of the inventions of the first, including railroads, the steam locomotive, and the steamship.

Together, the first and second industrial revolutions had a massive impact on economies and living standards. They are credited with lifting millions out of poverty, enhancing the quality of life, and expanding human lifespans. For example, the average life expectancy today in the developed world is more than double the 37-year average life expectancy in the early 1700s (Roser, Ortiz-Ospina, and Ritchie, 2019). But, if you look at what was going on at that time, it was a story about disruption and struggle.

The early industrial revolutions decimated the agricultural and handworker economies that had preceded them. Rural communities were destroyed, and the people who lived in those communities were displaced as populations migrated toward urban centers in search of work. Skilled craftspeople—many of whom had spent decades in apprenticeships—found themselves out of work because similar goods could now be mass-produced at much lower costs. Prior to the rise of the trade union movement in the mid-19th century, industrialization created dangerous work environments, sweatshops, child labor, and long hours for subsistence wages. All of these unanticipated consequences are similar to some of the struggles we're experiencing today.

The third industrial revolution, which began in the 1970s, included the rise of the semiconductor, the beginning of digitization with mainframe computing, and the automation of manufacturing. It was the beginning of globalization, with new technologies that allowed companies to disaggregate manufacturing and produce their goods virtually anywhere in the world. The combination of computerization, manufacturing automation, and increased globalization has meant increased opportunities in many developing countries. It also led to the rise of many high-skilled jobs in the United States, and is thus sometimes referred to as the emergence of a "knowledge economy." However, it also led to the decline of manufacturing in the United States, the loss of good-paying manufacturing jobs, and an economic decline across much of middle America.

## A FOURTH INDUSTRIAL REVOLUTION AND THE FOUR FORCES OF CHANGE

We are now in a "fourth" industrial revolution. It is further accelerating and expanding some of the trends we've seen in past stages. It is also introducing entirely new dynamics. I believe we can think of this fourth industrial revolution in the context of four forces of change:

- *Advanced Computerization*
- *Artificial Intelligence*
- *Mass Interconnectivity*
- *A Shrinking World*

**Advanced Computerization** is the rate at which computer technology has improved and is becoming integral to human society. Consider how many tasks we do on our smartphones every day, and often without a second thought. The apps you use on a daily basis to browse your Twitter feed or Instagram, update your LinkedIn profile, shop on Amazon, watch your favorite Hulu or Netflix show, and post to Facebook all require far more computing power than NASA used to send the Apollo spacecrafts to the moon. Today, the smallest computers perform tasks that would have been unimaginable

FIGURE 1

THE FOUR FORCES OF CHANGE

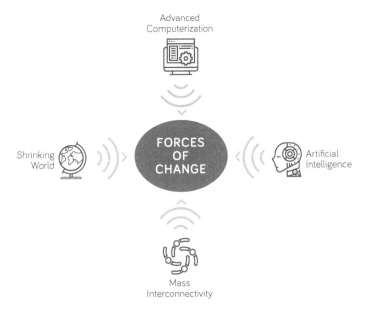

just 20 years ago, and our mobile devices provide access to a massive amount of human knowledge.

But computers are continuing to get faster, better, smaller, and cheaper. Newer technologies are on the horizon, and they have the potential to be millions of times more powerful—they'll make our current devices look even more antiquated than the punch card machines of the 1960s. On October 23, 2019, Google announced a major break-through: the world's first "quantum processor." (Gibney, 2019). Quantum computing is an entirely different approach to computing and one that promises to be millions of times faster and more powerful than the fastest machines we have today. The device that Google built took just minutes to perform a calculation that would take today's largest supercomputers 10,000 years to complete. Quantum computing is still in its infancy, and there are many technical challenges to overcome, but the technology is on the way. In the foreseeable future, computers will be even more integrated into our lives, accomplishing far more complex tasks—things we currently can't even imagine.

**Artificial Intelligence.** It's not just that computers are getting faster and better—they're getting "smarter" too. Artificial Intelligence (AI) has enabled computers to accomplish tasks that were previously thought to be uniquely human—unimaginable for machines—and computers are outperforming humans on some of these tasks. IBM's Watson supercomputer came to notoriety several years ago when it beat the world champion at Jeopardy! Since then, IBM scientists have focused on far more serious tasks, like oncology. Watson now has an accuracy rate of 90% in diagnosing lung cancer; the average accuracy rate for a human physician is only 50% (Steadman, 2013). That's because Watson is able to assimilate millions of patient records and other medical data—far more information than any human physician could review in a lifetime. Watson then develops its own understanding of how to identify cancer—a process called *machine learning*, which allows the computer to out-perform a human.

AI technology and machine learning are now being applied to a vast array of tasks—things like translating languages, autonomous self-driving vehicles, lip-reading, and facial recognition. Microsoft is even working on AI technology to help deliver certain types of psychotherapy (called cognitive behavioral therapy, or CBT) to improve outcomes for people suffering from conditions like depression and anxiety disorders (Belgrave and Thieme, 2019). One entertaining example of AI's rapid growth and vast potential is the Boston Dynamics autonomous robot, Atlas. Three years ago, Atlas could barely walk. In late 2019, Boston Dynamics released a video of this humanoid robot performing a gymnastics routine, including tumbling, splits, and twists, that a human gymnast would require decades of training in order to master (Porter, 2019).

As Google's CEO, Sundar Pichai, has said, "AI is one of the most important things humanity is working on," and that AI has the potential to be "more profound than electricity or fire." (McCraken, 2018)

**Mass Interconnectivity.** The third major force of change is about what the advent of technology has meant for how humans interact. Many people believe that technology has made people more isolated and lonelier. While that's true in some ways, there is another perspective: Thanks to the Internet, and our handheld web-devices, humanity is more interconnected than ever before. This interconnection has a host of ramifications, both good and bad. If you have a smartphone, you can make direct contact with anyone else on the planet who has an Internet-enabled device. As of the writing of this book, there are approximately 4.6 billion Internet users; that is almost 60% of the global human population (Clement, Global digital population as of July 2020, 2020). This means we can now share ideas more readily and with more people than ever before. But those ideas can also include things like fake news and hate speech. And there's another unanticipated outcome: those who don't have Internet access (40% of the world's population) face a serious opportunity gap (A. Wong, 2018).

Mass interconnectivity has already enabled entirely new business models, like Uber, Airbnb, and the self-publishing industry. It has caused the collapse of barriers to entry in countless industries, and it's enabled many entrepreneurs to bring novel ideas to market and compete toe-to-toe with industry giants. It has also caused tremendous disruption in long-standing industries (like taxi cab drivers, hotels, and traditional book publishers). As mass interconnectivity continues to increase, there will be an even greater impact on society.

**A Shrinking World.** One additional outcome of mass interconnectivity is that the world's geographical barriers are disappearing, creating a phenomenon known as "a shrinking world." This process began in the third industrial revolution (during the 1990s) when the advent of project management software, along with the early Internet, allowed complex projects to be disaggregated in smaller parts, so the work could be distributed across large geographies, possibly around the world. That provided economic opportunities for many poor regions of the world who had previously been shut out by geography. It also led to downward pressure on wages (and resentment) in rich countries like the United States. Today, the world is smaller than ever. Software platforms like Fiverr, 99designs, and UpWork™ allow freelancers from around the world to compete head-to-head in ways never seen before. The world of tomorrow will be even smaller.

## THE BIG DIFFERENCE BETWEEN TODAY AND THE PAST

At the time of the first industrial revolution, the average human life-span (in the United Kingdom, the epicenter of the industrial revolution) was approximately 37 years. The next major wave of change, the second industrial revolution, happened a century later. This meant that people living in that era had three human life-spans to adapt to the disruption. At the time of the second industrial revolution the average human life-span was still only approximately 40 years. It would be another 80 years before the next major wave of change (the third industrial revolution) so people still had multiple life-spans to adapt.

Today, with the fourth industrial revolution, things are very different. Change is happening at a much faster pace, there are simultaneous and overlapping waves of change, the average life expectancy in the U.S. is now 79 years (Center for Disease Control & Prevention, n.d.) and, as mentioned previously, we're working much longer. This means that people now need to adapt to multiple waves of disruption within a single human life-span. That's a major reason why today's disruptive change feels so daunting. It's also why cultivating a **Thriving Mindset** is critical.

## RESISTING CHANGE IS UNPRODUCTIVE AND DANGEROUS

In the early stages of the first industrial revolution (between 1811 and 1816), a group of textile workers—known as the Luddites—sabotaged factory machines and burned mills in resistance to the advancement in manufacturing. The Luddites were skilled artisans and craftspeople who blamed mechanization for forcing down wages and threatening their livelihoods. They also objected to the fact that factory looms allowed unskilled, un-apprenticed workers to take over their jobs, thereby devaluing the skills they had spent years developing. The Luddites feared that industrialization would ultimately destroy their communities and way of life. The parallels between the Luddites' plight and the concerns many people have about current-day advancement are striking.

The Luddites were correct about the threat, and their fears and grievances were, in some ways, justified. The early stages of the industrial revolution ushered in barbaric and exploitative labor practices and industrializing destroyed much of the craft-based artisan economy the Luddites depended on. However, their resistance to advancement was unproductive—and ultimately self-destructive. The act of "machine-breaking" was criminalized by the British Parliament and sometimes carried a death penalty (The Encyclopaedia Britannica, n.d.). The British military intervened on behalf of mill owners, many Luddites were killed, and the rebellion was violently crushed.

The cautionary tale from the Luddites' story is that, throughout human history, once the genie of advancement (and advancing knowledge) has been released from the bottle, there's no going back. This has applied to advancements like the wheel, fire, the steam engine, electricity, the computer chip, and, most recently, AI technology.

The Luddites were a case of an active, violent, and ultimately dangerous resistance to change. There are also more passive examples of resistance to change, and they too carry peril. These include people who might resist a corporate change initiative; or refuse to learn a new technology tool; or long to turn back the clock to a simpler, less tech-enabled way of life. The peril is that the rest of the world will continue to move forward (to learn, adapt, and evolve), while you remain mired in the past. People who are staunchly resistant to change ultimately find themselves left behind. Rather than meeting change with fear and resistance, a more productive perspective is to recognize that disruptive change always brings challenges. There are opportunities for people who can see past those challenges, thrive through the disruptions, and potentially come up with creative solutions to those challenges.

## WHY *THE THRIVING MINDSET* IS CRITICAL AT THIS MOMENT IN HISTORY

As in the past, the changes we see today are causing enormous pain for a lot of people. Some are responding to that pain by going down a dark path—one that's based on fear, and that taps into some of the worst parts of human nature. Luddite-like actions and reactions are surfacing again in today's environment, in a very dangerous way.

American manufacturing—which once formed the foundation of the American middle-class—has been on the decline since the 1970s. Many middle-American, "rust-belt" communities have been devastated by the decline. Workers in these areas grew up believing they'd have access to steady, good-paying jobs that don't require extensive education, just like their fathers—and perhaps grandfathers—had. Instead, they have watched helplessly as the factories that supported their communities for generations have abruptly closed. The economic damage is often permanent because there's typically no way to recover the scale of economic activity that has been lost. People in these communities—areas that comprise large swaths of the country—are left feeling abandoned, frightened, and angry.

That's what happened in Lordstown, Ohio, a community with a story that's become typical in middle-America. A small community in the northeastern part of the state, Lordstown was formerly home to a large General Motors (GM) assembly plant, which had been in operation since 1966. It was the largest employer in the county, at its peak, employing over 10,000 workers. However, the plant had been in decline (and reducing headcount) for two decades, as GM sought more cost-effective manufacturing solutions. In November 2018, GM announced that it would be eliminating all remaining jobs and closing the plant permanently (Tavernise, 2019). The plant closure was devastating to the community. It's estimated to have had an $8 billion impact on the local economy (Kalfman, n.d.), as the GM plant—even after years of downsizing—was still the largest employer in the area.

In 2020, there was some good news: a new company purchased the defunct GM plant—Lordstown Motors, a startup that builds electric pickup trucks (Domonoske, 2020). But the news wasn't all good: the jobs would not be returning at anywhere near the previous scale. The electric pickup truck was much simpler to manufacture, and the plant had plans to modernize to include far more automation.

The story that unfolded in Lordstown Motors (e.g., factories returning, but using fewer workers) is a typical story for modern-day manufacturing: production processes have been optimized to be much simpler, and therefore require fewer workers; much of the work is automated, and many of the jobs that are created are highly technical and require a college education. Studies have indicated that the vast majority of manufacturing job losses in the U.S. (approximately 85%) are due to advancing automation; only 15% are due to outsourcing and globalization (Hicks and Devaraj, 2015). Even though there has been a steep decline in factory jobs, manufacturing output in the U.S. has grown (Hicks and Devaraj, 2015)— that's because automation has allowed companies to produce more while employing fewer workers.

Despite the increase, there is still a false popular narrative that American jobs have been shipped to Mexico, China, and other global developing economies. That false narrative is a huge problem. It's a big part of what has led to a wave of resentment and a demand to restore a way of life many Americans viewed as their birthright—a way of life with the easily-accessible, good-paying factory jobs their parents and grandparents had. The resentment has unleashed some very dangerous forces— hyper-nationalism, racism, tribalism, anti-Semitism, and xeno-phobia are all on the rise (Hassan, 2019).

Just as with "machine breaking" by the Luddites two centuries ago (who resented the undermining of artisanal craftwork), the current day resentment (with the accompany-ing dangerous forces) is an ineffective response to disruptive change. It's misguided and self-destructive.

As history has shown, factory jobs weren't lost to Mexico, so much as they were lost to a microchip. We have vast portions of the American public who have been left behind by technological advancement, and who now lack the skills to be productive in an advanced 21st-century economy. In the coming years, there will be more pressure. By the year 2030, an additional 20 million jobs around the world could be displaced by automation (Oxford Economics, 2019). The four forces of change will also impact more middle-class workers, and even upper-middle-class workers, as technology becomes even smarter. The jobs of the future will require more knowledge, more sophisticated ways of thinking, and the ability to evolve and keep pace with change. (We'll talk more about this in Chapter 10, Building Intellectual Capital.) At the same time, American students' performance continues to decline in comparison to their international peers, especially in critical "fourth economic revolution" areas like science and math (Khalil, Jeff and Thompson, 2019).

We have some very big challenges ahead. We need to ensure that people are prepared for our ever-increasing technological prowess (e.g., the ever-increasing expansion of human knowledge), and ensure that those advances improve quality of life across society—not just for a privileged few. Descending into resentment, hate, racism, hyper-nationalism, tribalism, anti-Semitism, and xenophobia _will not_ provide the solutions we need. Those dark forces are actually a trap that will prevent us from finding solutions. They are an example of the kind of trap that prevents people from thriving; something I call the **Adversity-Fear-Paralysis Cycle**, which I discuss in Chapter 2.

It's also important to note that the complex problems we face require solutions in many domains—business, politics, economic policy, and social justice—most of which are beyond the scope of this book. (Some excellent titles that delve into these broader domains include, _Arguing with Zombies: Economics, Politics, and the Fight for a Better Future_, by Paul Krugman; _The World Is Flat: A Brief History of the Twenty-first Century_, by Thomas L. Friedman; and _Caste: The Origins of Our Discontents_, by Isabel Wilkerson.)

However, cultivating more people who have a *Thriving Mindset* is an essential part of the answer, which is what I will focus on in this book.

When people develop *The Thriving Mindset*, they can become part of the solution. That's why *The Thriving Mindset* is so critical at this moment in history.

We need individuals who can face up to the kinds of challenging and frightening problems we face, without descending into the dark side of human impulses. We need leaders who can guide people through the kind of disruption and uncertainty we face by appealing to the best within people, rather than by stoking fear and pessimism. And, we need to create a society that recognizes what unites us—our commonalities and interdependency—rather than being divided by difference.

## WHY I WROTE THIS BOOK

The time is clearly right for building the skills to thrive in the face of disruption and change, but that's not the only reason I felt called to write this book. Thriving through disruption is very personal for me because it is also the trajectory of my own life's journey. If you read my bio, you'll see that I run my own executive coaching business and that I've also had a long and successful corporate career at multiple Fortune 100 companies like Pfizer and American Express. You'll also see I earned an Ivy League undergraduate degree from Cornell University, as well as an MBA from New York University. But these accomplishments belie something else that is equally important. My bio doesn't talk about how I started out, which was as an African American man, born to a single mother, and in a very low-income New York City neighborhood in the 1970s.

It was a neighborhood where we were often afraid to walk the streets. Despite my mother working extremely long hours, we struggled financially and we frequently couldn't afford things like heat or electricity. In fact, sometimes we worried about losing our home altogether and winding up on those streets that we feared so much. It was an existence defined by disruption and uncertainty, to say the least.

According to a study by researchers at Stanford, Harvard, and the Census Bureau (Chetty, Jones and Porter, 2018), a young African American man, growing up in the circumstance I did, has approximately a six percent chance (Bradger, 2018) of moving on to the life that I've been fortunate enough to have (Bradger, 2018). When people hear this story and those odds, they often want to know what was the exact moment that things changed for me. In truth, there was no "magic moment." Things changed because of a lot of hard-won lessons in dealing with uncertainty, what it takes to overcome adversity, and ultimately, what it takes to thrive in the face of an extremely disruptive environment—lessons in cultivating *The Thriving Mindset*.

I tell this story because I would later find that those same lessons were also what made me successful in some of the most challenging corporate environments. And, I found that I could craft those early lessons, and many others throughout my career, into a set of tools and everyday practices to help others thrive.

The executive coaching business I now run focuses on sharing those tools and practices. This book is a compilation of the tools and techniques I've developed for cultivating a *Thriving Mindset*. They are based on my own experiences working in organizations that were going through disruptive change, and my experiences with the many individuals and companies I've had the privilege of helping in my executive coaching practice.

## A MESSAGE OF HOPE IN A TIME OF FEAR AND UNCERTAINTY

This book is intended as a message of hope. The coming years will bring many types of disruption, both in our personal lives and in our careers. A lot of people are scared. However, when you equip yourself with the right skills—the skills to cultivate a *Thriving Mindset*—you can turn disruption into an advantage.

## WHO IS THIS BOOK FOR?

People who will find the book useful include:

- Corporate leaders in organizations or industries undergoing disruptive change
- Entrepreneurs who need to lead businesses in the highly dynamic and uncertain start-up world
- Professionals whose companies are going through disruptive changes like mergers, acquisitions, re-organizations, or others kinds of change
- People taking on new job responsibilities that come with challenges, like a significant promotion
- People facing (or contemplating) a career change
- Professionals in a job search, and who face uncertainty about the future
- Business leaders who want to improve their organization's ability to thrive amid disruption, change, and uncertainty

- Anyone in a leadership position who needs to inspire others through changing or uncertain times
- Parents who want to provide their children with the best skills to navigate the changing and disruptive world they will inherit
- Educators at all levels who want to help their students better understand and thrive in an uncertain world
- Community leaders who want to help their constituents get past the fear and divisiveness that have become prevalent in today's world and to find their way through to courageous, real solutions

## WHAT YOU WILL LEARN

The book breaks the ability to thrive into specific principles or "dimensions" of a *Thriving Mindset* and explains how these dimensions can support personal and career development, as well as other basic parts of life. I provide case studies to demonstrate the power of each *Thriving Mindset* principle—real-world stories about successful people thriving through disruption, and those who weren't, and what makes the difference between them. I also offer personal perspectives from my own background and career. Here's a sample of what you will gain from this book:

- An understanding of what is at the root of thriving through disruptions, why some people are successful, and why others aren't
- A perspective on the kinds of disruptive change we're facing right now, what they mean, what's similar to disruptive changes in the past, and what's different now

- An understanding of the self-defeating cycle that traps a lot of people, why it prevents them from operating at their best, and how to break out of the cycle
- How to set a clear direction for yourself, one that will act as a North Star during the most uncertain times
- How to cultivate the resources that are needed for success
- How to think outside-of-the-box and innovate, even in the most challenging circumstance
- How to cope with failure
- How to lead others at times of disruption and uncertainty

## WHAT YOU'LL FIND IN THIS BOOK

There are eleven dimensions of **The Thriving Mindset**—each one detailed by a chapter in this book.

### FIGURE 2

### THE 11 DIMENSIONS OF THE THRIVING MINDSET

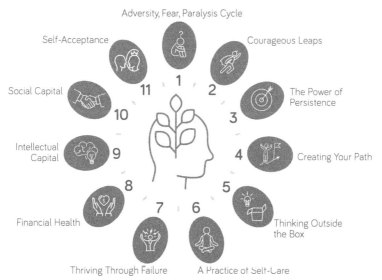

Adversity, Fear, Paralysis Cycle
Self-Acceptance
Courageous Leaps
Social Capital
The Power of Persistence
Intellectual Capital
Creating Your Path
Financial Health
Thinking Outside the Box
Thriving Through Failure
A Practice of Self-Care

**The Adversity, Fear, Paralysis Cycle & Courageous Leaps:** Chapter 2 explains the self-defeating cycle that many people fall into: *The Adversity-Fear-Paralysis Cycle.* This cycle acts as a kind of trap, and it prevents people from taking the steps necessary to thrive in the face of disruption. The chapter also explains what it takes to escape the cycle—a process I call taking Courageous Leaps.

**Understanding Courageous Leaps:** Chapter 3 goes deeper into what it takes to make a Courageous Leap. The chapter looks at the five stages of a Courageous Leap, and why some people get derailed—why they prematurely abandon opportunities, even after they took the first steps toward a promising opportunity.

**The Power of Persistence:** Chapter 4 explains a critical ability that we all can leverage, the Power of Persistence. You can think of the Power of Persistence as a force that catches you after a setback, and that supports you through struggles. The key is learning how to tap into that power within ourselves.

**Creating Your Path:** Chapter 5 explains one of the most important parts of thriving—understanding where you want to go. The chapter discusses a process I call "creating a path," and it explains why understanding your path is more productive than creating the "personal mission statements" that are so popular. The chapter also discusses why your path is not static, but rather something that evolves over time as you learn and grow.

**Trading in The Currency of Ideas:** Chapter 6 discusses one of the most important things for thriving in a disruptive world; the ability to generate ideas, to think creatively, and to innovate. I call it Trading in The Currency of Ideas. Many people struggle to think creatively, and most organizations recognize that innovation is in short supply. That's because most people are stuck in what I call "inside the box thinking." This chapter discusses what it takes to break out of that box, why outside-of-the-box thinking is so critical in the world that is emerging, and why most people get stuck "inside of the box" in their thinking.

**Building a Practice of Self-Care:** Chapter 7 explains why caring for yourself is a critical part of *The Thriving Mindset*, and why self-care is especially important at times of disruption and uncertainty. The chapter dispels some of the myths about self-care, explains why many people find themselves on a slippery slope of very poor self-care (especially at times of disruption and uncertainty), and outlines three important components of good self-care.

**Thriving Through Failure:** Chapter 8 discusses an important reality—when we stretch ourselves and strive to excel, there will inevitably be setbacks and failures. In fact, failure is almost always part of the process of achievement and growth. This chapter discusses how to persevere through the inevitable setbacks and how to cultivate a mindset that leverages failure as an asset for learning, evolution, and growth.

**Financial Health:** Chapter 9 discusses a topic that makes many people uncomfortable—money! The chapter dispels popular myths about money, explains the relationship between money and *The Thriving Mindset* (it's not what most people think), and examines a common pitfall that holds many people back—financial shame. The chapter presents a more productive approach to looking at money and an approach that helps people thrive—Creating Financial Health.

**Intellectual Capital:** Chapter 10 discusses another critical resource for making the Courageous Leaps that enable people to thrive—Intellectual Capital. The chapter defines what Intellectual Capital is; explains why Intellectual Capital is more important than ever, in the disruptive world that's emerging (the fourth industrial revolution); and looks at the four components that make up Intellectual Capital.

**Social Capital:** Chapter 11 discusses the third asset, Social Capital, that (in addition to financial health and Intellectual Capital) is critical for thriving. The chapter looks at why your social connections—or Social Capital—can make or break your ability to thrive in challenging times, and why Social Capital is especially important in today's fast-paced, dynamic, and hyper-connected world.

**The Journey to Self-Acceptance:** Chapter 12 looks at the final principle of a *Thriving Mindset*, and one that many people forget: in order to thrive, we must be able to accept and value ourselves. The chapter looks at how, when we look carefully enough, we can find hidden strengths within ourselves, and how—with self-acceptance—these strengths can open the door for tremendous opportunity.

## GETTING STARTED

To begin, let's look at where you currently are with each of the dimensions that make up *The Thriving Mindset*. In the appendix of this book, you will find a copy of *The Thriving Mindset Assessment*. This tool will allow you to identify your specific strengths and weaknesses across each of the dimensions. (You can also download a printable copy of the assessment form at the special website provided in the appendix).

After you complete the assessment, you'll know which chapters are most important for you, but I recommend you read all the chapters in the order provided. That's because the chapters are written to build upon one another. You will likely also discover helpful insights even in the areas of thriving where you are already strong.

Let's get started!

CHAPTER TWO

# BREAKING FREE OF THE ADVERSITY-FEAR-PARALYSIS CYCLE

## HOW PEOPLE GET STUCK

When faced with disruption, many people fall into a self-defeating cycle I call the *Adversity-Fear-Paralysis Cycle*. It happens when we let our fear-based instincts trigger destructive behaviors, and those behaviors cause a downward spiral into ever-worsening circumstances. Understanding this cycle—and how to break out of it—is at the core of **The Thriving Mindset**.

First, we need to understand that disruption is just a normal part of life. It might be the technology-driven disruption we're seeing right now, which—as we've discussed—is simply the result of advances in human knowledge. But disruptions come in many different forms—so much so that people don't always recognize when they're facing a disruption. Some common disruptions include:

- The loss of a job
- Getting promoted, starting a new job, or taking on a challenging project

- Getting a new or excessively demanding boss
- Moving to new areas
- Having to adapt to a new technology
- Launching your own company
- The birth of a child
- Purchasing a new home
- Getting married
- Getting divorced
- Uncertainty about your company's future

You will notice that some of the disruptions on this list are positive life events, but they are still moments that pull us out of our comfort zone, and thus are disruptions nonetheless.

We experience disruption as a kind of life adversity, and the normal response to adversity is fear—the fear that we won't be able to meet the demands of the adversity. For example, in the case of rapidly advancing technology, many people are afraid they won't be able to keep up. With the birth of a new child, many people worry about their ability to meet the demands of parenting.

But this fear isn't the problem. The problem is when we allow the fear to become a type of *"paralysis"*—which is an inability to respond productively to the disruption—and paralysis always leads to more disruption. Either the initial disruption gets worse, or a new disruption arises—that's when the self-perpetuating, downward spiral of the *Adversity-Fear-Paralysis Cycle* comes into play.

Here's one example of the cycle: Eastman Kodak declared bankruptcy in the year 2000, after over a century as an enormously successful company, and much of that time Kodak was the dominant force in their industry. Some would say the

FIGURE 3

## THE ADVERSITY-FEAR-PARALYSIS CYCYLE

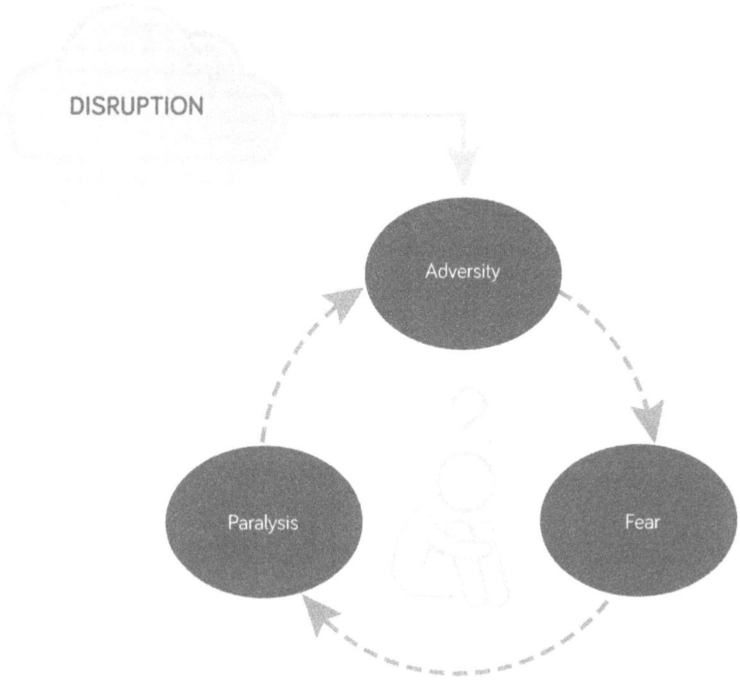

bankruptcy was caused by the advent of digital photography, but that explanation overlooks an important fact: a Kodak engineer by the name of Steve Sasson invented the first digital camera in 1975.

How could something like that happen; a successful company being undone by its own invention? It happened because Kodak fell prey to the *Adversity-Fear-Paralysis Cycle*. When faced with the disruption of a new technology (digital photography), Kodak's leaders (a group of men who only understood the film business) allowed their fear of change to cause a paralysis that prevented them from leveraging their own invention.

Sasson was quoted in a 2015 *New York Times* article recounting how difficult it was to get anyone at the company to pay attention to his invention (Estrin, 2015). In desperation, Sasson tried to get top management at Kodak to understand that his invention was about much more than just taking pictures. He explained that this new technology represented the first time visual images had been digitized and that the concept held enormous potential. In a statement that now seems prophetic, Sasson tried to convince the company that someday this invention "might even make it possible to send pictures over the phone line."

Kodak's leaders saw digital photography differently. They considered it a threat to the core of their business. At the time, most people took their pictures on Kodak film, and often in Kodak cameras; they had the film developed with Kodak chemicals, and they even had their pictures printed on Kodak paper. Kodak's leaders saw the digital camera as a threat to every step in the Kodak value chain.

When people fall into the *Adversity-Fear-Paralysis Cycle*, they become obsessed with surviving the disruption of the moment, and they fail to notice the opportunity that the disruption may also present. In Kodak's case, the company's leaders believed survival was about preserving the current state of the photography business, and so they resisted the technological advancement. They failed to see the opportunity that the disruption also presented; the opportunity to entirely re-imagine photography, and to see what the photography business could ultimately become. By the time Kodak leadership caught on, it was too late; the competition had an insurmountable lead, and the disruption of a new technology—one that was actually their own invention—ultimately lead to Kodak's bankruptcy.

## EXAMPLES OF ADVERSITY-FEAR-PARALYSIS ARE EVERYWHERE

Today, the shortsightedness of Kodak's leadership seems almost comical. After all, who better to lead in the photography revolution than Kodak? But similar examples of the *Adversity-Fear-Paralysis Cycle* are all around us, and most people don't recognize it.

It's the employee who is resistant to change, seeing change as a threat to his survival. It's the leader who is so frightened that she micromanages everything and paralyzes her team. The cycle can appear in your personal life—for example, with a friend who's gotten themselves into a bad position—maybe they're over their head in debt or in a bad relationship. They might say that they're trying to dig their way out. In truth, they're making one bad decision after another and making the hole that they're in bigger.

I saw many examples of the cycle during one of my job experiences in the Fortune 100 world: my 13-year tenure with Pfizer Pharmaceuticals. Since its founding in 1849 in Brooklyn by two recently emigrated German chemists, Charles Pfizer and Charles Erhart, Pfizer has become one of the world's most successful pharmaceutical companies. It's also a company that has faced the need to evolve, adapt, and innovate many times over the years in order to stay competitive.

I was hired by Pfizer during one of the times when they needed to evolve and adapt. It was just after the FDA had approved marketing of pharmaceutical products directly to consumers—rather than just to doctors—and Pfizer needed to quickly build a capability in direct-to-consumer marketing. I had experience with many other companies in the consumer marketing space, and was brought in to build out a new team in what would become Pfizer's consumer marketing department.

During my time with the company, I worked on several large-scale change efforts, including entirely new ways to market products, the introduction of new digital technologies, and reimagining how the company trained and managed its 12,000-person sales force. Pfizer also acquired a number of other pharmaceutical companies over a period of several years, an evolution which meant many corporate reorganizations, and that many staff roles became redundant. I witnessed more than 30 heartbreaking rounds of layoffs; sometime impacting long-term, dedicated employees who'd been with the company for their entire careers, and who hoped to be there through retirement. The work environment became a mix of exciting new opportunities, along with unsettling disruption.

One thing that stood out to me at Pfizer was that some people were especially good at coping with the challenges of the disruptive business environment. These were the people who were good at finding the opportunity in disruption, they were prepared to think in new ways, and they could thrive amid the disruption. They may have been just as afraid as anyone else, but they avoided getting caught in the *Adversity-Fear-Paralysis Cycle*. Sometimes the disruption meant they needed to leave the company. Even then, these were the people who would quickly land on their feet, often finding significantly better positions elsewhere.

## HOW TO BREAK OUT OF THE ADVERSITY-FEAR-PARALYSIS CYCLE

Here's the most important thing to remember about the *Adversity-Fear-Paralysis Cycle*, and it's something that people who have **The Thriving Mindset** seem to know instinctively:

> *There's nothing wrong with being afraid; it's what you do when you're afraid that matters.*

You can learn to see the fear that naturally comes with life's disruptions as a sign that you're also standing in front of an opportunity. Thriving is about learning to use that fear as a source of excitement, and as a kind of springboard to evolve and leap toward the opportunity that typically accompanies disruption.

I call it taking a *Courageous Leap*. Cultivating **The Thriving Mindset** is ultimately about learning to find and take those *Courageous Leaps*.

### FIGURE 4

### COURAGEOUS LEAPS

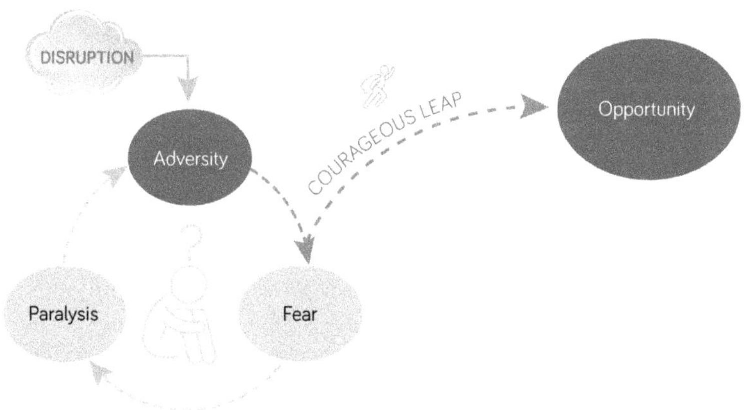

## A COURAGEOUS LEAP OUT OF A TOUGH SITUATION

In 2011, a woman named Melanie Lockert graduated from New York University with a master's degree in theatre arts. She was also saddled with enormous educational debt— nearly $100,000, including interest payments (K. Wong, 2018). Like many young people entering the post-2008 recession job market, Lockert struggled to find employment, and ended up working a string of minimum wage jobs. Despite working long hours, she struggled financially and found herself with little money left to pay off debt. Some of her lowest points included going without health insurance and, for a short time, relying on the Supplemental Nutrition Assistance Program, also known as "food stamps." She feared what her financial troubles would mean for her long-term life prospects (like owning a home) and she struggled with feelings of guilt and shame about her situation. She wondered if her finances were ultimately a reflection of personal inadequacy.

Lockert had many reasons to be afraid, but she didn't allow her fear to turn into *paralysis*. Instead, she took a very interesting *Courageous Leap*. She faced up to her fears by starting a blog (DearDebt.com) to chronicle her experience with overwhelming debt. Initially, the blog was a tool to keep herself accountable for making responsible financial choices. Over time she attracted a significant following, and she found that there were large numbers of young people with the same struggles. Lockert even learned that some people found her blog by searching, "I want to kill myself because of debt," which alarmed her. She came to understand the complexities of debt and that many people conflate their self-worth with their net-worth. She realized that getting out of debt involved more than just good discipline; it's also about coping with issues like self-esteem, guilt, shame, and depression. These are things that most authorities on personal finance weren't addressing. Lockert saw an opportunity.

Today, Lockert has successfully paid off her student loans, but she's also accomplished much more. She's established herself as an expert in personal finance. She's published a book, *Dear Debt: A Story about Breaking up with Debt,* and she's co-founded the Lola Retreat, which helps women gain financial literacy, face their fears about money, and gain control over their financial lives. Lockert has also become a mental health advocate and organizes an annual Suicide Prevention Awareness event in the U.S. to share resources for people struggling with thoughts of suicide because of debt.

Lockert's achievements are substantial: she's a published author, she's established herself as an expert in personal financial management, and she's launched programs that are helping thousands of young people achieve financial success. It is safe to say that Lockert has achieved far more than she would have, had she not encountered disruption. Lockert epitomizes the principles of *The Thriving Mindset*: She didn't just "survive" in spite of disruption; she evolved, grew, and accomplished even more *because of* what she experienced.

### THE THRIVING MINDSET: KEEPING YOUR HEAD UP AND FOCUSING ON GROWTH

The difference between what Lockert achieved, and the fate that befell Kodak illustrates two essential parts of developing a *Thriving Mindset*: Keeping your head up (not down) and focusing on growth.

When under stress, many people default to "keep your head down and get the work done." While it's true that continuing to get work done during times of disruption is important, keeping your head down is often a path into the *Adversity-Fear-Paralysis Cycle*. A heads-down posture typically sacrifices learning and growth.

You could argue that Kodak was already thriving. They'd been in business for more than a century. They had led many prior advances in photo technology, including new types of cameras and film, and they were an extremely profitable company. In theory, there were in the ideal position to take a heads-up view and re-imagine what photography would ultimately become.

But they didn't do that. Instead, Kodak took a *heads-down* posture. They focused on continuing business as usual, and they stuck to what the company knew best: chemical-based photography. Kodak saw themselves as the industry leader, and they believed all they needed to do was keep working in the old way. They assumed photography would, largely, stay the same as it had been in the past. Sure, there would be incremental advancements, but they believed the company would continue to lead the advancements, as they had done in the past.

Kodak's heads-down view constrained the company's thinking so much that it caused them to misunderstand the core of its business. Kodak's leaders believed they were in the film, camera, and photographic chemical business. In reality, they were in the "memories" business—they helped customers capture and share memories. When a better technology came along to meet customers' needs—one that didn't depend on film and chemicals—customers left for the better technology.

A heads-up posture would have given Kodak a very different perspective. Digital technology was driving disruptive change in many industries, and photography was no exception. A heads-up posture that focused on growth would have allowed them to see digital photography as an opportunity, rather than as a threat, to reimagine the company's business model, and to better envision what digital photography would ultimately become.

Melanie Lockert's response was the opposite of Kodak's. When Lockert first encountered her disruption—graduating into a recession, with substantial student debt, and struggling to find employment—she too was at risk of falling into the *Adversity-Fear-Paralysis Cycle*. The biggest danger was the misalignment between her internal perceptions and the external reality: her belief that her struggles somehow reflected personal inadequacy rather than the broader economic reality.

Launching the blog was the key—it was a step toward lifting her head up, finding an opportunity for growth, and changing course towards an opportunity that also accompanied the disruption she was facing. The blog aligned her perceptions with the larger external reality. She learned that she was far from alone in her struggles. In fact, many people were having even more serious problems. Lockert recognized that there was an opportunity: the financial planning industry wasn't meeting all the needs of people like her, and she had something important to contribute. Instead of feeling constrained by her challenges, she could be excited about the value she had to contribute. It was the kind of opportunity that significant disruption often presents, if you lift your head up so you can see it.

## CHAPTER SUMMARY—PUTTING IT ALL TOGETHER

In this chapter, we discussed how people get stuck at times of disruption and how they can start to break free.

### Some Key Points to Remember

- Disruption and adversity are just a normal part of life. Many disruptions are negative events, like the loss of a job or a difficult financial situation. However, even positive events—like the birth of a child or a job promotion—can be experienced as a kind of disruption.

- The natural response to disruption is fear, the fear that we won't be able to meet the demands brought on by the disruption. That's perfectly normal; however, the problem comes when people allow their fears to turn into a kind of *paralysis*—which is an inability to respond productively to the disruption.

- The reason people get stuck is because of a self-defeating cycle: the *Adversity-Fear-Paralysis Cycle*. This cycle is what prevents people from thriving when faced with disruption. The danger of this cycle is that it tends to be a self-perpetuating, downward spiral because *paralysis* always leads to more adversity—either the initial gets worse, or a new adversity arises.

- Breaking free evolves recognizing that *there's nothing wrong with being afraid; it's what you do when you're afraid that matters*. You can learn to see the kind of fear that naturally comes with adversity as a signal that you're also standing in front of an opportunity. You can learn to use that fear as a kind of springboard to leap out of the

*Adversity-Fear-Paralysis Cycle* and into the opportunity. We called that taking a "*Courageous Leap.*"

- Thriving through disruptive times is all about learning to see and take those *Courageous Leaps*. The following chapters will focus on building the skills to take those *Courageous Leaps.*
- Being able to take a *Courageous Leap* often means taking a heads-up posture when you face disruption (rather than a heads-down posture) so that you are able to see opportunity.

## Key Questions to Think About

Think about the following questions to start putting these ideas into practice.

1. When have you observed someone in the *Adversity-Fear-Paralysis Cycle*? It might have been someone else or yourself; it could even be an entire organization, like the Kodak example we discussed.
2. What new adversities arose as a result of the person being caught up in the cycle?
3. What is one example of a *Courageous Leap* you've observed someone take at a time of disruption or adversity?

# CHAPTER THREE

# UNDERSTANDING COURAGEOUS LEAPS

Several years ago, I met a young woman named Cindy, who struggled with the idea of *Courageous Leaps.* She was in the midst of a very tough time in her career. At her previous job with a high-tech firm, she'd felt under-appreciated and under-valued and had grown tired of the struggles of being a woman in a male-dominated industry. She'd decided to make a career change to something that felt more meaningful, where she would be valued. A year and a half before we met, Cindy had taken a new job with a non-profit. Cindy's new employer was an organization in the social services sector, and the organization's mission really appealed to Cindy's personal values. She'd taken a pay cut—even though her new position was more senior—but she believed the cut was well worth it to do something more meaningful.

But a year and a half into this new job, Cindy was still unhappy, although for very different reasons. She no longer felt as under-valued, but her new organization had (in her words) "a whole different kind of crazy" that she hadn't anticipated and was ill-prepared to handle. Once again, she was miserable.

When I talked with her about the *Adversity-Fear-Paralysis Cycle* and *Courageous Leaps*, she said she'd already done all that. She believed the move to a non-profit had been her *Courageous Leap* towards a vision of a new opportunity. In her words, "the vision didn't come true."

Cindy was right about having taken a *Courageous Leap*. But she didn't understand the full challenge that's often involved in making a *Courageous Leap*. It's a problem that a lot of people encounter, and one that often takes them back into a state of *paralysis*.

## MAKING A COURAGEOUS LEAP—THE FIVE STEPS

Making a *Courageous Leap* usually isn't a *single*, simple step. In fact, *Courageous Leaps* are typically made up of five steps. It's a process that includes both ups and downs— some steps may take more time than you initially expect, and the process always includes uncertainty, challenge, and growth. It's important to understand that taking a *Courageous Leap* is a process. If you don't, you run the risk of misinterpreting what's going on and potentially becoming discouraged, which often causes a relapse into the trap of *paralysis*.

Cultivating **The Thriving Mindset** isn't about just making that first leap—it's about having the stamina and persistence to progress through all five stages so that you can ultimately achieve the new opportunity. The five steps of a *Courageous Leap* are:

1. *Envision & Leap*
2. *Fall*
3. *Struggle*
4. *Evolve*
5. *Achieve*

**FIGURE 5**

**THE FIVE STEPS OF A COURAGEOUS LEAP**

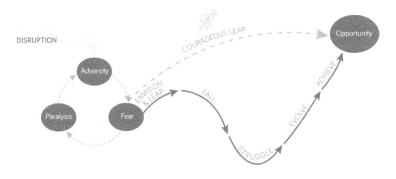

## STEP 1: ENVISION & LEAP

It's exciting and exhilarating when we take action towards a new opportunity—that first leap toward something you may have envisioned and planned for a long time. It might be the feeling when you start a new job—the "honeymoon" period. Or, the feeling of starting a new business. Perhaps it's a leap we've envisioned for years and the exhilaration is about finally turning the plan into a reality. That first leap can be even more exhilarating if it's a leap out of the place of fear.

Cindy told me how excited she'd been when she found the non-profit she'd joined. Initially, it seemed like the place she was always meant to be. But as is often the case, Cindy's initial excitement was short-lived.

## STEP 2: FALL

For most people, there's a feeling of "free-fall" sometime between 30 and 90 days after taking the initial leap, even in an extremely well-planned *Courageous Leap*. This is when the honeymoon period at a new job ends, or when you discover the realities of running your own business are far more challenging than you'd expected. In Cindy's case it was when she discovered her new industry had "its own kind of crazy," one she couldn't have anticipated. The Fall is usually jarring and unsettling. Some people describe it as that feeling in the pit of your stomach when riding a roller-coaster. Remember, the Fall stage is a natural part of taking a *Courageous Leap*, and it's also important. In many ways, the Fall sets you up for the real growth that comes from a *Courageous Leap*.

## STEP 3: STRUGGLE

The Fall stage is important because it's what takes you into step 3—the Struggle. Struggle is the most productive—and the most perilous—of the five stages. The Fall stage reveals the full realities of the leap you've taken. The Struggle stage is where we reckon with those realities. In Cindy's case, Struggle meant understanding the realities of the non-profit she'd joined. Although the organization's work was important to her, there were some very significant challenges in the organization's culture, challenges that were much more daunting than she'd anticipated. The Struggle stage is also where we learn. Often, it's a level of learning that would not have been possible before taking the leap, because we're learning about things that were beyond our ability to envision before.

But there is also a serious risk during the Struggle stage. Many people give up on their *Courageous Leap* in the midst of the struggle. I call that "foreclosing" on the opportunity. Foreclosing often causes people to drop back into the *paralysis* part of the *Adversity-Fear-Paralysis Cycle*. That's what happened with Cindy. She was crushed by the experience of hoping for a better career, taking the leap towards that opportunity, giving up money in the process, and then being so disappointed in her new position. She was just hoping to go back and get a job somewhere in the tech industry. She had resigned herself to being unsatisfied and miserable at work—she just wanted the higher paycheck to go along with the misery. It was devastating to hear the extent to which she'd given up on her vision and, in many ways, also given up on herself.

## STEP 4: EVOLVE

There can be a much better outcome to the Struggle phase: when the effort of struggling causes us to learn and evolve. Struggle can be seen as a "crucible," where our work experiences and the elements of who we are, interact to forge something new. The Evolve stage is where that "something new" starts to emerge.

Sometimes we learn we have more strength within ourselves than we'd originally imagined, and therefore are able to overcome the additional hurdles involved in achieving the opportunity we pursued. In that case, the "something new" that evolves from the crucible of struggle is a stronger sense of self. Other times, struggle causes us to make a shift in our plans. Rather than pursuing the exact objective (e.g., opportunity) we had in mind, we make a slight shift and pursue a slightly different path. The new path might be one that's even more fulfilling than the initial one.

For Cindy, I recommended that she consider the lessons to be learned from the career change she'd attempted. Sometimes taking stock of the lessons learned is what opens the door to evolving after the struggle that can follow a *Courageous Leap*. At first, Cindy said that she'd learned to "never leave a good-paying job", but Cindy was wise enough to know there was more, much more, available to her. After more reflection, she realized that she'd gone into her new role with rose-colored-glasses. In truth, there was no way any job could have lived up to the idealized scenario she'd envisioned. That was important because it pulled Cindy out of a victim role and into a more active role. Over time, she realized that the "craziness" of her new industry wasn't a fate that had befallen her but rather (at least partially) a disappointment she'd set herself up for by anticipating nirvana. The realization allowed her to step back and be more objective and balanced toward the non-profit sector and her challenges. In Cindy's case, the ability to step back and be more objective was an important part of her evolution.

## STEP 5: ACHIEVE

The 'Achieve' step is where the pay-off happens. It's when we get to *live into* the new opportunity, whether it's the same opportunity we'd initially envisioned during our first leap or a new opportunity that came into focus through the Struggle and Evolve stages. This is also the step many people start to "re-envision" another (often higher) opportunity. That's because when you reach the Achieve stage, you're literally looking at the world around you from a higher level, with the additional knowledge and perspective that you gained in the Struggle and Evolve stages. In these cases, people often follow the Achieve stage by taking another *Courageous Leap*, and the process starts over again.

For Cindy, Achieving meant deciding to give her new non-profit organization another year while at the same time focusing on being more neutral (and less idealistic) in her expectations. Essentially, she was deciding to give her new organization a fair shot, rather than holding them up to an unrealistic ideal—the ability to achieve this was her real *Courageous Leap*. Cindy admitted that she was a person of very tightly-held ideals, and having patience with employers had never been her strong suit in the past. Building that level of patience was a critical asset she needed to create the future she wanted, whether at her current non-profit organization or elsewhere.

## MY FIVE STEPS JOURNEY WRITING THIS BOOK

One of my most significant personal experiences with *Courageous Leaps* was writing this book. A decade ago, I would never have envisioned myself writing a book. In fact, I didn't consider myself a writer at all, and hadn't taken an English class since high school. I never imagined I'd be drawn to writing, much less that I'd be good at it. But I came to understand that having a book is important from a business perspective for someone in my industry, as many executive coaches and public speakers have books on the market.

Originally, I planned to write a purely business book on "resilience," one that was highly technical and didn't include many details about my personal life. I took the first *Leap* of this process when I drafted the book concept and the introductory chapter and sent my work to ten close friends for review and comment.

The Fall came almost immediately after I pushed the "send" button. These are ten people whom I deeply respect. They are very intelligent and highly accomplished. What if this idea was so ridiculous that it caused them to lose respect for me? I was wracked with uncertainty and terrified of the embarrassment that I worried could follow. It was definitely that pit-of-your-stomach feeling as the rollercoaster crests the big hill. A part of me wished I could pull the document back.

The Struggle and Evolution came when I got the feedback. My friends were uniformly supportive, kind, and encouraging. Some of them even remarked that they hadn't known how good a writer I was—that was a huge boost! But there was also challenging feedback. Not that I shouldn't be doing the book, but rather that I needed to go deeper, better differentiate the project from work that's already been done, and make the book more personal.

The several months that followed were a combination of learning, evolving, and sometimes falling back down into the crucible of struggle. One key struggle was to better understand the topic that *really* interested me. What unique insight did I want to provide to the world? The idea of making the book more personal was an even bigger struggle. My 27 years in the corporate world had left me more comfortable hiding behind a shield of technical business ideas. I was terrified of just being human and vulnerable, talking openly about things I had long considered to be personal flaws, and things that I had worked for most of my life to conceal. I was also scared of talking about some of the painful parts of my family story and discussing mistakes I'd made along the way. That fear can be common among people from disadvantaged backgrounds who are trying to climb to a higher rung on the socioeconomic ladder. We believe that we have to present a facade of perfection and that we can never allow the scars from our journey up the ladder to show through.

But I evolved. I came to understand that my personal story—flaws, scars, and all—is the important part. My story, including the painful parts, is what ultimately made me successful, especially in times that were disruptive and uncertain. The mistakes I'd made along the way were important lessons that should be shared.

Struggling, learning, and evolving helped me re-envision the book. I recognized that the book I wanted to write was a candid combination of what I'd experienced in my journey, what I've gained from it, and why that journey is relevant to thriving amid disruption.

## CHAPTER SUMMARY—PUTTING IT ALL TOGETHER

In this chapter, we looked more closely at *Courageous Leaps*, and we examined what it takes to make a *Courageous Leap*.

## Some Key Points to Remember

- *Courageous Leaps* often aren't just a single, simple step. They are more complicated and typically involve five separate stages: Envision & Leap, Fall, Struggle, Evolve, and Achieve. Cultivating **The Thriving Mindset** is about developing the ability to successfully make it through all five stages.

- One of the things that prevent people from thriving in the face of disruption is that they give up too quickly, especially during the Fall and Struggle stages of the *Courageous Leap*.

- The Fall stage can be especially daunting, even frightening. It's the stage of the *Courageous Leap* when reality sets in, and you start to realize that there's more involved in making the full leap than you might have initially envisioned. For example, if the *Courageous Leap* involved taking a new job, the Fall often occurs after the first few months when the proverbial "honeymoon" period ends, and you learn the more challenging parts of your new organization.

- The Struggle stage is where people reckon with the reality of the full leap they want to make. People who are successful persist through Struggle and into the Evolve and Achieve stages. This is where the real progress happens! For people who are willing to put in the work, Evolve is where they learn and grow. Often, Evolve launches people into a level of achievement that is beyond what they originally envisioned when they first conceived of the *Courageous Leap*.

In the next chapter (*The Power of Persistence*), we'll take a look at some of the skills you can put into place to help you successfully make it through the demands of the five stages.

## Key Questions to Think About

Think about the following questions to start putting these ideas into practice.

1. When was a time that you tried to take a *Courageous Leap* (i.e., to make a significant change) and found out the change was going to be much more challenging than you'd originally anticipated?
2. Were you successful at making it through all five stages of the *Courageous Leap*, or did you give up on your original idea?
3. If you persisted, what were some of the things that helped you through the difficult times?
4. Or, if you didn't persist, what lessons did you gain from the experience?

CHAPTER FOUR

# THE POWER OF PERSISTENCE

$F$alling after you leap can be terrifying, and sometimes there's a lot at stake. The key to surviving the Fall is tapping into a very specific ability that we all can leverage: the *Power of Persistence*. You can think of the *Power of Persistence* as a force that catches you during the Fall, lifts and supports you through the Struggle, and helps you move into the Evolve stage. The *Power of Persistence* is also a critical part of **The Thriving Mindset.**

## THE POWER OF PERSISTENCE: A GIFT FROM MY MOTHER

I first learned about the *Power of Persistence* by watching my mother. There are many negative stereotypes of Black single mothers in America: that they're "welfare queens" looking for a hand-out, that they're irresponsible, or that they're lazy drains on our country's resources. My mother was one of the

FIGURE 6

THE POWER OF PERSISTENCE

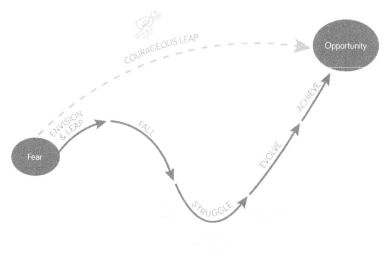

THE POWER OF PERSISTENCE

hardest working people I've ever known. She shouldered far more than her share of responsibility, often at great hardship and cost to herself. She never sought or received a handout, and over her lifetime, she contributed *far more* than the country she was born into ever gave her.

This is not to say that she was perfect. Not by a long stretch. In fact, after I became an adult, much of our relationship was strained and painful. Among other things, she never fully accepted me as a gay man, or when it came time, accepted my marriage. She was a *very* proud and strong-willed woman and had some tightly-held, traditional views. I am a *very* proud gay man, equally strong-willed, and progressive in my thinking. Two strong-willed people of radically different viewpoints, will not always find common ground. However, our differences on that front do not diminish my admiration of her strength, my gratitude for how hard she worked, or my appreciation for what I believe to be the "gift" of persistence I inherited from her.

My mother came from circumstances most people could never fully imagine. She was born in 1929 in a small rural town in the segregated, Jim Crow-era South. Most people only think of segregation as "whites only" drinking fountains and being forced to ride in the back of the bus. Although true, those things don't begin to reflect the full horror of the American South in that era and the dangerous world my mother was born into. It was a place where a Black person could be brutalized, tortured, or murdered for *any* challenge to the racial system: things like failing to step off the sidewalk (and into the gutter) to yield the way for a white person on the street; looking a white person directly in the eye; or failing to address them as sir or ma'am (Black people were only ever addressed by their first names). Violence could befall a Black person if they advocated for better education, higher pay, or better working conditions. Schools were strictly segregated. Black schools were woefully underfunded and under-equipped. Some only went to the 8th grade, making a high school education unattainable. With the exception of the historically Black Colleges and Universities, southern colleges and universities were "whites-only." African Americans were prevented from voting. In some areas, it was illegal for a Black person to testify against a white person in a court of law. It was a world where African Americans were relegated to the most menial jobs, often lived in terror, and had no avenue to advancement, economic opportunity, or justice of any kind.

It was also the world my mother would escape. Her escape is an excellent example of a *Courageous Leap*. The determination it took to make that leap impacted her views for the rest of her life. My mother was part of what historians call the Great Migration, which was a period between 1916 and 1970 when six million African Americans fled segregation in southern states in search of the freedom and equality they believed they could find in the North and other parts of the U.S. (Wilkerson, 2011). In my mother's case, this meant leaving the small town she'd been born in, heading first to Detroit, and later to New York City. She faced many struggles throughout her life, but she also ultimately earned a license as a registered nurse, purchased a home, and raised two children—all while sending much-needed money back to her parents and siblings in Virginia. Growing up, I can remember how much we struggled financially, and yet many of my mother's relatives faced much harder circumstances. She believed it was her responsibility to do whatever she could for them, as well.

There was another disruption in my mother's life. I have a brother who is six years younger than me. My brother had extreme behavioral problems as a young child, and in early adolescence, he was diagnosed with schizophrenia. Schizophrenia is a serious mental illness with symptoms that can include delusions, visual and auditory hallucinations, and highly disordered thinking. In extreme cases, symptoms can also include violent behavior. There is (sadly) no cure for schizophrenia, only management. Treatments are woefully inadequate, often consigning the person to terrible side effects. The disease is often totally debilitating, to the point that people with schizophrenia comprise much of the homeless population. Out of respect for my brother's privacy, I will not delve more into his specific circumstances in this book, other than to say that, managing a child with an incredibly severe mental illness was another disruption my mother faced.

Leaving the segregated South did not free my mother from the marginalization of being a Black person in America. She would also face the struggles of being a single woman raising two children on her own, the gender bias of being a single woman in the 1960s, and the extraordinary challenge of having a child with a debilitating mental illness. The thing that allowed her to survive was her steely determination: persistence and perseverance were fundamental parts of her nature. She would often say, "Whenever someone says you can't do something, make it your job to prove them wrong." It's advice I watched her demonstrate many times. I once asked her how she gained the courage to leave her hometown alone, leaving everything she'd known behind. She said the decision was simple. She'd watched her own mother live a life that was limited to legally-enforced servitude—scrubbing floors and cleaning other peoples' homes. My mother refused to "be anyone's maid."

There are important lessons about *The Thriving Mind-Set* in my mother's story. First, my mother had envisioned a *Courageous Leap*, out of the segregated South and into opportunities in the North. She'd also decided what was most important to her: the refusal to live under the limitations her own mother had endured. That was a critical part of her *Power of Persistence* because, when you experience the fear of the Fall and the Struggle, it's critical to know your priorities. My mother's world was filled with disruption and uncertainty, but there was no "giving up." Her only option was to go forward, no matter what it took.

I've had many colleagues and friends comment that, when I want something, I develop a laser-like determination. I don't have to think hard to see that it came from my mother. It's been a tremendous gift at times of disruption and uncertainty.

## THE FAT KID, THE SOCCER TEAM, AND THE POWER OF PERSISTENCE

Here's a story about how the *Power of Persistence* came into my life at a very early age: As a kid, I was severely overweight. By the time I was in 9th grade, I weighed well over 250 pounds. Being overweight is much more common for kids from low-income neighborhoods (Borrell, Graham, and Joseph, 2016). Some studies have shown that kids from low-income homes have double the obesity rate of those from high-income families (Center for Disease Control, 2019). That's because poor kids often don't have safe places to play and be active, and they lack access to nutritional food. Low-income areas in the United States are often "food deserts," meaning that the neighborhoods lack access to fresh and healthy foods.

My weight had always been a source of shame, and the ridicule from other kids was relentless. Like most people who are overweight, I'd tried virtually every diet available. None worked. When I started high school, I decided to try something new: I went out for the school's soccer team. To be clear, I went to a very small high school that wasn't known for athletic talent, and soccer wasn't a popular sport. Basically, anyone who wanted to be on the soccer team got a spot.

I also had another reason for joining the team: I was an extremely lonely and isolated kid, and I desperately wanted to fit in. This was a small private school, and I was there on a scholarship for economically disadvantaged kids. Most of the other students came from privileged families, and there were very few Black kids. I carried a lot of shame about being from a poor neighborhood, the condition of our home, and about being the son of a single parent. This was in the 1970s, and there were still very strong norms about the traditional two-parent family. I had very few friends and virtually no social life, and I wanted to change that.

But joining the soccer team didn't help my social life. In fact, it made matters much worse. The white soccer coach had nothing but disdain for a fat, Black kid who had the audacity to join his team. He couldn't kick me off the team (because I was showing up for all the practices), but he took every opportunity to ridicule and humiliate me. The practices were torturous. Each one started and ended with a mile run. I was carrying 250 pounds on a 15-year-old, 5'6" frame. Those runs weren't only exhausting, they were painful. The coach had no sympathy and never offered encouragement. Worse yet was playing practice games as "shirts and skins." Shirts and skins was a way of signifying two different teams by having half the boys take their shirts off. Those practice games meant I had to run up and down the field shirtless and deeply ashamed of how my body looked. The other kids would laugh, and again, the coach had no sympathy.

The worst part came on the game days. For an entire season, the coach never put me in to play a single minute in a single game—no matter how hard I'd worked in practice or how far ahead we were in the game. He let every kid play except me. I would show up on time for every game, put on my uniform, and hope this would be the time when I finally got the chance to at least feel like part of the team. It never happened.

A lot of people might wonder why my parents didn't intervene. But that's another reality about being the scholarship kid from a single-parent, low-income family. My mother was working insane hours just to keep us afloat. She didn't have time to come to soccer games and see what was happening, and I was too embarrassed to complain. There is no question that the coach would have behaved very differently had I been one of the wealthy white kids, with parents who had the time and resources to offer protection.

Something else important happened in the 9th grade. That was the year I was moved up to an accelerated math class. Although I lacked athletic talent, I was very good at math and science, and the school recognized it. Moving into this class was an enormous opportunity. It meant I could take the school's most advanced math curriculum, and that would put me in an excellent place for college admissions.

But the soccer coach was also the advanced placement math teacher! I stood out just as much in that class as I did on the soccer field. I was the only Black kid, the only fat kid, and the only low-income scholarship kid. And the teacher had the same disdain for me in class that he had for me on the soccer field. Within the first week, he told me I didn't belong in his class.

But there was also an important difference between the soccer field and the classroom. I was a very good student, *and I knew it.* I was more than capable of keeping up with the class. And math has an added benefit. Answers are either right or wrong, and the teacher doesn't have much latitude in grading. As time went on, no matter what he said, I knew I could learn the material and get the right answers on tests. Truth be told, the fact that I could stand up to him in math class (which was far more important to me than soccer) gave me the strength to persevere through all those tortuous soccer practices. I never missed a math class (and never missed a soccer practice), turned in every assignment on time, and continued to do well on every test. At the end of the year, the teacher had no option other than to give me an honors grade. In the process, I also learned to never give up.

But the story didn't end there. Flash forward 21 years later, during the final miles of my first Ironman-Distance Triathlon—the first of eight I've successfully completed. By that time, I'd lost the excess weight, and I'd learned (much to my surprise) that I was a decent athlete. Finishing an Ironman is extraordinarily difficult. It's a 2.4-mile swim, followed by a 112-mile bike ride, and a 26.2-mile run. Even world-class elite athletes talk about how tough the event can be. But to me, finishing the Ironman wasn't all that bad. That's because completing the 140.6 miles (all under my own power) could never be as excruciating as being the lonely fat kid, bullied by a malicious adult. The *Power of Persistence*—something I'd first learned from my mother, and later had to use on that soccer field and in the classroom—taught me that you can succeed in the things you want, as long as you don't give up.

## THE POWER OF PERSISTENCE IN THE BUSINESS WORLD

The "never give up" lesson I learned from my mother, and honed in high school, has supported me well beyond those early days. It's been especially valuable in the business world, with my career, and when I've been faced with some kind of professional disruption. It's been there every time I've had a difficult boss, whenever someone doubted me, and whenever I've faced something that seemed like an insurmountable obstacle. One of the most important times came at an early and vulnerable stage in my career.

In my mid-twenties, having earned my MBA and now beginning my corporate career, I'd landed a fantastic job at a very prestigious company in New York City. I was ecstatic about the job and proud of myself, especially since I was making more money than I'd ever imagined. It was an incredibly competitive environment, with enormous demands and extreme hours, but I was completely up for that. During the first few years, things had gone well, and I'd been promoted twice. Then, after a department reorganization, I landed with the ultimate "nightmare boss." For the sake of this book, I'll call him Sam, which, of course, is not his real name. In my nearly three-decade corporate career, I never again encountered anyone like Sam. He was a bully with a terrible temper and a horrible reputation for mistreating his employees. Like my soccer coach, he delighted in publicly berating his employees. His feedback always included personal attacks and never any kind of constructive guidance. Sam seemed to take an immediate and highly personal dislike to me. It might have been because I was out about being gay at work.

Since this was the 1990s, it was much less common than it is today to be out in the office and not always considered a protected enforced right. It also might have been because I was one of the very few Black management-level employees, but I'll never know for sure.

About six months after I started working for Sam, I got very sick. At first, I thought it was just a bad cold, so I didn't take any time off from work, largely because the pressure was so intense and everyone lived in fear of Sam's wrath. One day I became so sick and was coughing so hard, with stabbing chest pains, and felt so feverish that I had no choice but to leave the office. I went directly to an emergency room. An x-ray revealed that I had pneumonia. The doctors prescribed antibiotics and told me that I had to stay home and rest. If I didn't, I'd end up in the hospital. I relented and took the time off.

After a week at home, I felt well enough to come back to work. When I returned to the office, I discovered that Sam had spread a rumor that I had AIDS. There was nothing I could prove, but a couple of friends in the office let me know what was going on. This was early in the HIV/AIDS epidemic, at a time when there were no effective treatments, and when people living with HIV faced horrible discrimination. Co-workers might refuse to be in the same room with someone who was known to be HIV+. Sometimes people with HIV/AIDS lost their jobs due to fear and stigma.

I did not have AIDS. In fact, I was HIV negative. I had gotten seriously ill because I was working incredibly hard, under enormous (Sam-induced) stress, and often not sleeping. But more importantly, suppose I actually had been facing a life-threatening illness like HIV/AIDs? What Sam did could have been disastrous.

I was lucky. Despite the ultra-competitive corporate culture (and Sam's appalling behavior), it was a fairly progressive company. There were good non-discrimination policies, and there were other out gay people in the organization. Over time, the rumors largely settled down. Some friends and co-workers thought I should just quit. Surely, no job was worth enduring someone like Sam. He clearly had some kind of personal vendetta and was willing to sink to unbelievable levels. But the situation was more complicated. I had two very prestigious degrees, but I also had a mountain of educational debt. I hadn't yet amassed much savings, and I had no family resources to help me. I wasn't willing to take the risk of quitting without another job in hand.

I also had the *Power of Persistence*. Looking at my predicament through older and wiser eyes, I'm now also aware of two things I hadn't done for myself. I hadn't put enough emphasis on creating *"Financial Health"* (a concept I'll discuss in Chapter 9), so I was tremendously reliant on this job and vulnerable to someone like Sam. More importantly, I hadn't created enough *"Social Capital"* (a concept I'll discuss in Chapter 11), so I didn't have a network of people I could approach for advice and help in managing Sam.

But the *Power of Persistence* I'd first learned from my mother and later honed in those soccer days had made me tough. I was more than capable of withstanding a bully like Sam. I was determined to get solid work experience that would make me highly marketable and build enough savings so I wouldn't be held hostage in a job like this again. That was my number one priority. I'd even set a stretch goal of building a full year of living expenses in my savings account. I didn't yet understand **The Thriving Mindset**, but I knew my priorities and they were much more important than whatever Sam could dish out.

In the end, I got what I wanted. I saved a ton of money. I learned, I evolved, and I got great experience for my resume. I ultimately moved into another department within the same company, and to a much better boss. That new job also came with a promotion, an even better salary, and it would ultimately set me up for an even better move a couple of years later.

It was a classic example of a *Courageous Leap*, a Fall, Struggling, and (thanks to the *Power of Persistence*) learning to Evolve and Achieve. The *Courageous Leap* was moving into the Fortune 100 corporate world. No one from my family had ever landed a job like that—it was truly foreign territory. The Fall came a few years later when I ended up with Sam, and the Struggle went on for two years. But the *Power of Persistence*, and my focus on my key priorities, provided me with what I needed to ultimately Evolve and Achieve.

## CULTIVATING YOUR POWERS OF PERSISTENCE: FIVE KEY PRACTICES

Unfortunately, there are many bosses out there like Sam. You may find yourself with one of them after making a *Courageous Leap* into a new job. Likewise, many people who envision an exciting opportunity, maybe starting a new company, moving to a new region of the country, or going back to school and launching an entirely new career, find themselves dealing with a Fall and Struggle when that new opportunity doesn't pan out as expected. That's what happened with Cindy, the high-tech sector leader we discussed in the last chapter.

In all of these cases, cultivating your *Power of Persistence* is the key to surviving the Fall, and persevering through the Struggle, so that you can ultimately Evolve and Achieve. There are five key practices that allow you to cultivate your *Power of Persistence*:

1. **Know Your Priorities.** When you Fall after taking a *Courageous Leap*, it's critical to have a clear understanding of your priorities—what you are trying to accomplish. That's because your priorities become a kind of "*North Star*" that guides you through the Struggle. When my mother left the South, her priority was to build a life with opportunity. When I struggled through my days working for Sam, my priority was to create a better life for myself. Without clarity of priority, people often become lost and overwhelmed, and prematurely give up on their objective. (In Chapter 5: *Creating Your Path*, we'll talk more about establishing a clear idea of what you seek to accomplish.) When you experience the inevitable Fall after the initial leap, clarity on your priorities serves as a source of strength and motivation, a guide to get back on track.

2. **Name Your Fears.** The fall that comes after the initial part of a *Courageous Leap* is often terrifying. Just like I discussed in Chapter 2 (*The Adversity-Fear-Paralysis Cycle*), there is nothing wrong with being afraid—it's what you do when you're afraid that matters. The same thing holds true for the fear after you start to Fall and Struggle. I believe the most effective strategy is to name the fears. That means describing in detail exactly what you are afraid will happen. When you name and describe

a fear, it transforms the fear from a vague emotion into a concrete problem to be solved or a risk to be mitigated. For example, when Cindy (in Chapter 3) entered her Fall stage, she felt completely overwhelmed by the challenges in her new non-profit job. Her biggest fear was that she was going to be perpetually unhappy at work, never finding a job that suited her. Naming that fear transformed it from a vague feeling into a problem to be solved. That's what allowed her to move into a more active role and to look more carefully at what she was bringing to her job situations.

3. **Decide What's More Important Than Your Fear.** Here's something that the people with the greatest *Power of Persistence* are able to do: they decide what's more important than their fears. In fact, I believe the quality of courage is not about the lack of fear, but rather a decision about what's more important than your fears. One of my favorite examples of this kind of courage is Pakistani women's rights activist Malala Yousafzai. At a very young age, Yousafzai became an outspoken advocate for the rights of young women in developing nations, especially the right to an education. At age 15, Yousafzai was critically injured in an assassination attempt and suffered a gunshot wound to the head. Undeterred, Yousafzai continued her advocacy work (Nobel Prize Foundation, n.d.). She has spoken about her fear of another attack; but she has also spoken about how fighting for every girl's right to an education is more important than her fear. She went on to create an international movement and became the youngest Nobel Prize laureate in 2014 (Nobel Prize Foundation, n.d.).

Fortunately, most of us will never face circumstances like what Yousafzai faced when we take a *Courageous Leap*. But we are all capable of deciding what is more important than our fears.

4. **Learn to Stick With Things You're <u>NOT</u> Good at Doing.** There was another valuable lesson about the *Power of Persistence*, and it's something that harkens back to my high school soccer team experience. It's the value of sticking with something you're not good at doing. Conventional wisdom in professional and leadership development holds that it's best to focus on your natural strengths or passions and get support on (e.g., delegate or outsource) the things that are not your strengths. I agree with this idea for the most part, but with one important caveat: there is value to be gained from sticking with things that you're not naturally good at doing.

First, the effort and discipline needed to stick with something that is a struggle for you will build your *Power of Persistence*. Second, persevering through a struggle can also reveal talents that you didn't know you had. Both of these happened in my high school soccer experience: The level of effort and discipline needed to stick with soccer made other challenges seem minor. Even though I was naturally talented at math, there were times when even that didn't come easy. At the same time, the hurdles were very minor in comparison to soccer.

Struggling through soccer also helped me learn and ultimately discover a latent passion. Though I didn't have the dexterity that soccer required, I learned I do have a passion for outdoor sports and for endurance athletics.

That's why I was so drawn to running, cycling, and tri-athlons later in life. It was very difficult to see clearly in my soccer days, but my passion for outdoor sports was probably a big part of what helped me make it through the Struggles. Another way of thinking about it is that operating outside of your comfort zone, and sticking with it long enough, broadens your perspective. It's this broadened perspective that provides the increased knowledge that later becomes useful.

5. **Find Your Rocket Fuel.** There's one more tool I've found for building the *Power of Persistence.* I call it your "rocket fuel." One of the traditions at my high school was a luncheon for graduates and their parents immediately after the ceremony. The school is very small (there were only 47 graduates in my class) so people knew a lot about each other. During the lunch, my friend Shawn and his mother greeted my mother and me. Shawn's mother said, "I hear Gerry is going to Cornell next year." My mother said, "Yes, we're all very happy." Shawn's mother said, "I'm sure you are—and happy for 'affirmative action' too, I guess." With that, she excused herself and walked away. My mother and I were shocked.

Here's the backstory: Shawn, who was white, had also applied to Cornell, but he hadn't been accepted. He'd been accepted to another excellent college, but Cornell had been his first choice, and he was devastated. Shawn's mother was suggesting that the reason I'd gotten the coveted spot—the spot that to her mind Shawn had been denied—was because of preferential treatment I'd received as a member of a minority group, not because of talent or hard work. I strongly suspect that affirmative action had played some role in my admission—as had my grades, excellent academic record, and extremely hard work.

But here's what Shawn's mother had missed—and to quote former First Lady, Michelle Obama—"there are many kinds of affirmative action." There's the affirmative action of "legacy," like when colleges give preference to the children or grandchildren of alumni. At Harvard University, for example, the admission rate for legacy applicants is 33% versus the average admission rate of less than 6%. Similar disparities exist across many elite colleges (Gross, 2019). There's also the affirmative action of being a star athlete. And of course, there's the affirmative action of coming from an intact home, with two well-educated parents, and with plenty of financial resources. Shawn's mother was a college professor, and his father was an engineer—excellent people to help him along the way. Shawn and his parents divided their time between two homes—one in the most expensive neighborhood in Brooklyn, and the other, their weekend country home. My mother struggled by herself just to keep our rundown home in a poor neighborhood, and she was in no position to help me with academics.

Another student in my class also went to Cornell. He was white, and he was a "third-generation legacy," meaning that <u>both</u> his father and grandfather were Cornell alumni. He and Shawn were close friends, and their families had very similar economic advantages.

However, people (including Shawn and his mother) congratulated him for continuing the family tradition. There were no disparaging remarks about the "advantages" he'd received.

Soon after graduation, I learned that Shawn was also saying I'd be lucky to last the semester at Cornell. We didn't stay friends (for obvious reasons), but here is what did last long after graduation day: the remarks that Shawn and his mother made have become a powerful motivator, a kind of rocket fuel. It's true; there were some very demanding days ahead of me at Cornell. My classmates were some of the brightest, most talented engineering students in the country—at the time, Cornell's engineering school was ranked in the top five nationally—and the competition was intense. But no matter how tough it got, I always remembered Shawn and his mother. Their remarks were my motivator—my rocket fuel to work even harder and to fly higher.

No matter who we are, what our race, what we look like, or where we come from, most of us have had the experience of being pulled down—often by incredibly disparaging and hurtful statements from someone whom we trusted, looked up too, or someone who was in a position of power. I call these people the *destructive detractors* because there's no positive intent in their statements. Your destructive detractors are most likely to appear at the moments when you're stretching yourself—when you are attempting to achieve something remarkable. The secret is to transform the negative energy in their statements into your motivator—your rocket fuel.

## CHAPTER SUMMARY—PUTTING IT ALL TOGETHER

In this chapter, we looked at an essential capability for navigating through the Fall that inevitably comes after making a *Courageous Leap*: *The Power of Persistence*.

### Some Key Points to Remember

- As we discussed in Chapter 3, the Fall after a *Courageous Leap* can be terrifying, so much so that it causes many people to prematurely abandon worthwhile aspirations.
- You can think of the *Power of Persistence* as a force that catches you during the Fall and Struggle stages of the *Courageous Leap* and lifts you into the Evolve stage.
- Cultivating your *Power of Persistence* involves five key practices:

  1. **Know Your Priorities.** Understanding your priorities—the thing you are ultimately working towards—protects against becoming overwhelmed or disheartened.

  2. **Name Your Fears.** Just as I discussed in Chapter 2 (*The Adversity-Fear-Paralysis Cycle*), there is nothing wrong with being afraid—it's what you do when you're afraid that matters. The same is true for the fear that people experience during the Fall stage. Naming your fears and detailing specifically what you're concerned may happen allows you to transform the vague feeling of fear into a specific problem to be solved.

  3. **Decide What's More Important Than Your Fear.** Courage isn't about an absence of fear. Many

extremely courageous people are very conscious of their fears; they simply decide that something else is more important than the fear. Once you understand your priorities and name your fears, you're in the position to take charge of your fear by prioritizing something else. That's a critical part of making your way through Struggle and into Evolve.

4. **Learn to Stick With Things You're <u>NOT</u> Good at Doing.** It feels good to work in an area where you're already proficient, but that isn't the optimal environment for growth. Successfully achieving *Courageous Leaps* often means having the resolve to persist through the discomfort of sticking with something that you're not yet good at doing.

5. **Find Your Rocket Fuel.** No matter who we are, we will all face *destructive detractors* at some point—people who deliver destructive and counter-productive comments when we are stretching towards an important goal. The key is to transform the negative energy into your rocket fuel, and to use it as a motivator.

## Key Questions to Think About

Think about a time when you were able to persist in something that you were not good at doing.

1. How did it feel to be out of your comfort zone?
2. What did you tap into that helped you persist through the challenge?
3. How might you tap into that ability on other occasions?

CHAPTER FIVE

# CREATING YOUR PATH

$Y_{our\ Path}$ articulates how you generate value in the world. As part of normal day-to-day life, we are consumers—the food we eat, the water we drink, the things we purchase and use, the services other people provide to help and support us, etc. Understanding how to balance what we consume with the value we generate is a critical part of **The Thriving Mindset.**

In my professional career, I've found that focusing on my path, rather than simply getting consumed by the disruption of the moment, has made me more fulfilled and happier. In my work as an executive coach, I've seen that when people take the time to formulate a path and consider how they generate value, it increases their ability to thrive through disruption.

## YOUR PATH IS UNIQUE TO YOU, AND IT'S DYNAMIC

It's important to remember that the way you seek to generate value in the world is unique to you and your priorities.

FIGURE 7

CREATING YOUR PATH

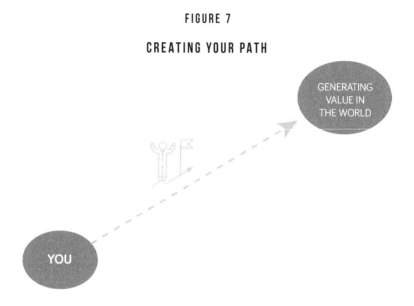

For some people, generating value might mean an audacious contribution, like curing cancer, ending climate change, or eliminating poverty. For others, generating value might be a much more modest achievement, like providing their children with access to a college education and more opportunity. For the purposes of cultivating a *Thriving Mindset*, all paths are equally valid. What's important is whether the path you've articulated generates sufficient value for you.

*Your Path* may also evolve over time. We'll talk more about how paths evolve, and why that's an excellent thing, later in this chapter.

## MORE VALUABLE THAN A PERSONAL MISSION STATEMENT

*Creating Your Path* is more valuable for cultivating a *Thriving Mindset* than the notion of a personal mission statement—what some people call their "purpose." Personal mission statements borrow from the idea of company mission statements. They are typically concise and succinct, consisting of only one to three sentences, and they can be valuable for aligning and inspiring a group of people. Consider Google's mission statement: "*To organize the world's information and make it universally accessible and useful.*" It's easy to see how this concise statement helps create alignment across a global organization.

However, concise mission statements can also be one-dimensional. Focusing on a personal mission statement, instead of a path, doesn't adequately support the complexity of decisions that individuals face when we need to navigate disruption.

## THE SEVEN MILESTONES THAT DEFINE YOUR PATH

Understanding and articulating the path that is right for you means looking at the seven components that frame and define *Your Path*. I call them the seven milestones.

1. **Professional and Personal Goals.** What personal and professional goals would you like to achieve? These might include specific jobs or titles you want to achieve during your career, like becoming the CEO of your company, or founding a start-up or non-profit organization. From the personal goal standpoint, they might include things like creating a supportive home environment for your children, climbing a mountain, or earning a Ph.D.

2. **Interests and Passions.** What are the things that interest you? What are you passionate about in life? Try thinking

FIGURE 8

**THE SEVEN MILESTONES THAT DEFINE YOUR PATH**

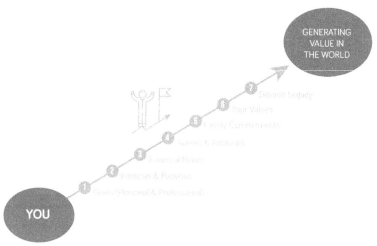

about what problems or challenges you see in the world that you would like to work toward solving. These problems might be large or small, depending on your interests. Some people have a passionate interest in the environment or a particular social justice cause. Other people have a passionate interest in the arts or a creative endeavor. Your interests and passions can be an intersection across multiple areas.

3. **Financial Needs.** What are your financial needs? This might include supporting yourself in the way that you would like, but also any other financial commitments that you may have. It's important to keep financial needs front and center because they are an important reality-check (and maybe deciding factor) for the direction that *Your Path* can take. We'll also discuss the concept of *"Understanding Wealth & Creating Financial Health"*

in Chapter 9, which forms an important intersection with the financial needs milestone on *Your Path.*

4. **Talents and Aptitudes.** What talents and aptitudes do you have to offer in your quest to bring value to the world? This can be a very broad category, including areas where you have formal training (e.g., law, business, or the sciences) as well as informal or soft skills, like being a good communicator, artistically creative, or a good networker.

5. **Family Commitments.** What family needs and commitments do you have that are important to you? These are parallel to the financial needs we discussed earlier but are broader in nature. You may be a parent and have a financial commitment to child care (in addition to family financial needs), or perhaps you are caring for aging parents. As with financial needs, it's important to keep family commitments front and center because they too can form an important reality-check or deciding factor.

6. **Values.** What personal values do you use to hold yourself accountable? These shouldn't be idealistic, nice-to-have items, but rather the things you are willing to make sacrifices for. A good litmus test is whether you would be willing to give up money (or something else of significance) in exchange for that value. If not, it probably isn't really one of your values. These values might also include any religious or spiritual beliefs that impact how you live your life.

7. **Desired Legacy.** What legacy would you like to leave behind? Desired legacy, of course, has a relationship to professional and personal goals, but its broader. Legacy is about the value that will endure after you are gone.

A great question to ask yourself is: What do I want people to say or remember about me?

## YOUR NORTH STAR AMID THE STORMS OF DISRUPTION

Some of my clients have described the pace of today's disruption as feeling like a ship at sea, caught in the midst of a storm. They feel like they're being hit by multiple waves at the same time, and as if the waves are coming from different directions. The most frightening part is that they feel like they're always down in the trough of the waves, with no visibility—no way to see the whole storm. At these times, a well-articulated path acts as a kind of *"North Star."* It helps people focus on the bigger picture, puts immediate challenges into perspective, and helps steer them to the right decisions, so they stay on course toward what's most important.

## CASE STUDY: CREATING A PATH THROUGH DISRUPTION

When Charles engaged me as his executive coach, he was facing a big question: Should he make a significant career change? The question had huge ramifications for both him and his family. At the time, he was feeling exhausted, overwhelmed, and somewhat direction-less, thanks to some difficult times at his company.

Charles was a senior technology leader for a company in the healthcare and medical devices field. He had started his career as a programmer many years ago, and he had worked his way up to the vice president level. By most measures, Charles had done very well. He was a multi-talented individual with a wide range of interests. In addition to being a senior technology executive, Charles was also a skilled woodworker and artisan. He spent what little spare time he had in his home workshop, making sculptures and high-end furniture for friends. In fact, prior to his technology career, Charles had seriously considered starting a high-end woodworking business. But in light of his family obligations, he decided to go the corporate route.

The company Charles worked for was enduring a long period of chaos. There had been multiple rounds of restructuring, re-organizations, and layoffs. It was a highly disruptive environment, in all the worst ways. Despite the uncertainty, Charles was well-respected in the company. But his reputation hadn't protected him entirely, and on top of it, he had also shouldered the unenviable task of laying off many talented people over the previous two years.

The turmoil had left Charles feeling burnt-out and uncertain about his future. He was contemplating leaving the company and going out on his own, perhaps as an independent consultant. He also considered making a significant change and starting the woodworking business he'd contemplated long ago. Charles had been very happy in his corporate career for many years, but things had changed dramatically. He was one of the people who described the feeling of being caught in a "storm of disruption."

Charles and I spent several weeks working on his path, and it ultimately provided the answers he was seeking. All of the seven path milestones yielded important information, but there were three milestones that proved especially important for Charles. They were *Family Commitments, Financial Needs, and Desired Legacy.*

**Family Commitments:** Charles was very happily married, and he had three daughters, ages 13, 11, and 9. Charles' wife was a registered nurse. She had taken time off from her career after their first daughter was born, but she had resumed work once all three children were in school. Charles' family was his highest priority. He loved being a father, and he wanted to be the best possible parent and husband. In fact, that was one of the reasons Charles was considering a career change. He was concerned that the stress of work was taking a toll on his family. In addition to working extremely long hours, Charles was also bringing some of the stress home with him. Once home, he wasn't able to engage and interact with his family the way he wanted to.

**Financial Needs:** There was an overlap between the family and financial commitment milestones on Charles' path. Charles and his wife provided a very stable home and financial life for their family. They had made good financial decisions and (for the moment) their finances were in very good shape. However, this didn't necessarily extend to their future, and it didn't fully support the family's goals. Charles and his wife wanted to provide their daughters with a high-quality college education. They were on schedule with saving, but they needed to continue at that pace in order to hit their goal. Charles' wife was in a high-demand field, so her income was reliable. They could afford a minor disruption in Charles' income, but not a long-term loss of income—which was actually one reason the volatility at his company made him so uncomfortable. However, looking at the financial commitment milestone helped Charles realize that a highly volatile field (like consulting or starting a business) was too risky for his goals.

**Desired Legacy:** Examining Charles' desired legacy revealed another angle that brought the full picture together. There were three important parts of the legacy Charles wanted to leave behind. He wanted to be remembered first, as an excellent father—one who provided for his family's long-term well-being, both financially and personally. Second, Charles wanted to be seen as a problem solver and a "creator." At first, this seemed to support his plan to go into consulting or start a woodworking business—but there was a twist. The third part of Charles' desired legacy was that he wanted to be seen as generating large-scale impact. He realized this was part of why he'd sought senior roles in the corporate world: climbing the corporate ladder allowed him to deliver on an ever-increasing scale of impact. Charles realized that being an independent consultant, or running a woodworking business, wouldn't provide him with the scale of impact he desired. Even if he were financially successful, these avenues would be too limiting.

Here's the picture that ultimately arose: Charles' current career path was right for him, but his current company was not. The volatility was beyond his level of tolerance, and he'd lost confidence in some of the senior leaders at the company.

Charles made the decision to continue his career in corporate technology leadership, but to initiate a job search. We worked together for several months more as Charles implemented a search strategy that was ultimately successful. He stayed in the healthcare industry but moved to a larger and more stable company. He also got a very significant compensation increase in the process, which he and his wife funneled entirely to increasing their savings. Charles was now leading a much larger department, so he also had more impact than before.

As with any senior-level job, there were stresses and challenges, which Charles experienced in his new position, but because the environment had improved, these weren't a problem for him. Charles now sees overcoming the challenges as part of delivering the scale of impact he desires. The key to thriving through the disruption of his prior company was that Charles needed to better understand his desired path and get back on that path.

## YOUR PATH WILL EVOLVE OVER TIME

There is one more important part of understanding *Creating Your Path*: you need to regularly revisit your seven milestones, consider any things in your life that may have changed, and adjust *Your Path*. Humans are dynamic beings, we learn new things along our journeys, and we evolve. It's therefore natural that our paths evolve and that we may set new priorities.

Charles was a great example of this. He realized that his path would likely shift when his children complete their education. At that point, his financial needs and family obligations will shift, and he may want to revisit the idea of starting his woodworking business.

I typically recommend that people dedicate time at least once a year to revisit their path and reassess their own seven milestones.

## CHAPTER SUMMARY—PUTTING IT ALL TOGETHER

In this chapter, we discussed how having a clear understanding of *Your Path* can help with making *Courageous Leaps* at times of disruption or uncertainty.

## Some Key Points to Remember

- *Your Path* is an articulation of how you seek to generate value in the world.
- During times of disruption or uncertainty, having a clearly articulated path can help people see their way through to the right decisions and thereby make the *Courageous Leap* that is right for them. You can think of *Your Path* as a *North Star* that helps keep you on course during the storms of disruption.
- There are seven milestones to consider in understanding *Your Path*:
  1. **Professional and Personal Goals.** What you want to achieve in your career and personal life.
  2. **Interests and Passions.** The things that you are interested in or passionate about in life.
  3. **Financial Needs.** Things like supporting yourself and your family in the way you would like, and any additional financial obligations you may have.
  4. **Talents and Aptitudes.** The specific talents and aptitudes you have to offer in your quest to bring value to the world.
  5. **Family Commitments.** The family needs and commitments that are a priority for you and that may constrain some of the options you have available.
  6. **Values.** The personal values you hold yourself accountable to—not idealistic, nice-to-have items, but rather the things for which you are willing to make sacrifices.
  7. **Desired Legacy.** The legacy you hope to leave behind and that will endure in the world.

## Key Questions to Think About

1. What are the three most important things that you want to accomplish? These could be professional goals, highly personal goals, or a combination of both.
2. What are your three top values—i.e., the things you value and that you are willing to make sacrifices for, so that you can have what you want in your life?
3. How might keeping these two lists at the top of your mind (i.e., keeping them as your *North Star*) help guide you in times of disruption or uncertainty?

CHAPTER SIX

# TRADING IN THE CURRENCY OF IDEAS

In Chapter 1, we discussed the *Four Forces of Change* that are at work today; how they are driving us towards a fourth industrial revolution; how this new industrial revolution includes a disruptive pace of change that is faster than anything seen before in human history; and the extraordinary pressure that this disruptive pace of change places on both individuals and organizations to either evolve and adapt, or be left behind. However, there's a very significant up-side of this fast-paced, disruptive pressure: *There's also never been a better time for creative and innovative ideas.*

Technology is making it easier than ever to implement new ideas, speed to market is increasing, and industries are hungry for creative and innovative thinkers. As this world enters this fourth industrial revolution, ideas can be thought of as a form of currency. People who can *"trade" in this* new *Currency of Ideas*—the ones who can bring new ideas to the table, articulate those ideas well, engage with others to refine and evolve those ideas, and ultimately take those ideas forward into action—will be the ones who excel in this new era. That ability to *Trade in The Currency of Ideas* is a fundamental part of **The Thriving Mindset**, because it unlocks the ability to make *Courageous Leaps* into the new opportunities that emerge in tandem with change and disruption.

## A FAILURE AT TRADING IN THE CURRENCY OF IDEAS

Many years ago, I had a work relationship that got off to a rocky start. It was with a colleague named Christopher, and the tension between us was ultimately about the ability to *Trade in The Currency of Ideas*; or, more accurately, the lack of that ability.

I had recently taken a position as a director of marketing at a mid-size publishing company. Christopher was the editorial director on my line of the business. The product Christopher and I worked on was a collection of hard-to-find books, published in a series at very high production standards—printed on very high-quality paper and in beautiful leather-bound editions. You could think of it as a "book of the month club" for bibliophiles.

My team was responsible for bringing in customers. Christopher's team was responsible for identifying which books we would carry and ensuring high-quality production of those titles. In theory, he and I shouldn't have been in conflict.

The problem started during a lunch we had in my second week on the job. During our conversation, I mentioned an article I'd recently seen about publishing books on computers. Bear in mind, this was 1994. It was the year IBM introduced the ThinkPad 775CD, the first notebook laptop with an integrated CD-ROM, and the year that Netscape introduced its first web browser, Netscape 1.0. Netscape was the forerunner of Firefox, Google Chrome, and Safari. It would still be many years before the iPads and Kindles we take for granted today appeared.

I thought "electronic books" were a fascinating concept, but Christopher was appalled. I'll never forget the look on his face or his response. He said, "I just can't imagine a world where, as a child, I'd have been deprived the pleasure of lying on the couch, with a fine book, and having a whole world of knowledge unfold with every turn of the page." Not realizing the hornet's nest I'd stepped into, I tried to clarify. I asked, "Wouldn't it be even better if you could open a whole world of knowledge with every click of the mouse?" (At the time, most people used desktop computers.) "That way, you wouldn't be limited to just one book at a time," I continued. Christopher was even more appalled. He changed the subject, and the rest of the lunch was very chilly, as was our working relationship thereafter.

In fairness to Christopher, he and I were from very different backgrounds. He was 20 years my senior. He'd been in the traditional publishing industry for decades, and was a true bibliophile. Christopher had built a career as an "old-school" editor, and he loved everything about physical books. He wasn't particularly comfortable with computers and was even a little suspicious of newer technologies. My interest in the idea of electronic books took something he loved (books) and marred it with something he distrusted (computers).

I wish that early lunch with Christopher had gone better, but of course, we all know how the story has unfolded: computer technology has reinvented the publishing industry, eBooks (and audiobooks) are now the norm, and the Internet and self-publishing have disrupted the publishing industry in ways no one had yet imagined in 1994 when Christopher and I were having lunch.

There were two reasons why that lunch conversation—one that I thought was so fundamentally interesting—went so poorly. One reason was on my side of the table: I was trying to bring Christopher into an exchange about an idea he found extremely uncomfortable. I wasn't yet as good as I needed to be at communicating innovative ideas, especially to someone for whom that idea might be uncomfortable. It's always important to remember that *Trading in The Currency of Ideas* is a two-way street; not only do people need to be receptive to new ideas, but the person communicating the idea needs to be adept at painting an inspiring and compelling vision. Over the years that followed, I put a lot of effort into learning how to frame ideas in a compelling story.

The other problem was on Christopher's side, and sadly, it's a very common problem. He had an extensive understanding of the traditional publishing industry, he was a very skilled editor, and he'd invested many years in honing his expertise. He was extremely knowledgeable, but his knowledge base was static, not dynamic—meaning that, despite his extensive expertise, he didn't invest in exploring ideas that were outside of his familiar domain. In fact, as I would learn during the time Christopher and I worked together, he was often hostile towards new ideas that were outside of his comfort zone. Christopher was very uncomfortable with *Trading in The Currency of Ideas.*

## BOXED-IN THINKING

A major reason why people can struggle with *Trading in The Currency of Ideas*—and even become hostile to new ideas—is something I call "Boxed-In Thinking." In the time we worked together, I learned that Christopher was a prime example of this dynamic, and it explained the hostility that would often emerge when he was presented with something that made him uncomfortable.

I use the term "boxed-in" (and the idea of a four-walled box) as a metaphor for this dynamic because the walls of the box represent four behaviors that act as limitations on thinking—defensiveness, thinking in terms of problems (rather than solutions), close-mindedness, and blame.

### FIGURE 9

#### Becoming Boxed-in

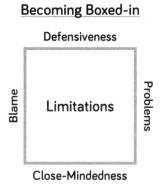

**Defensiveness.** When we take a defensive posture, we believe we're guarding ourselves against attack. When Kodak's executives shelved digital photography technology, they believed they were defending their business from a potential threat.

**Problems.** When we think in terms of problems (rather than solutions), it's a way to avoid having to take on new, potentially frightening challenges. For example, when confronted with a new idea, some people will instantly list all of the problems with that idea—all the reasons why it can't be done—in an attempt to shield themselves from the risk of having to engage with that idea.

**Blame.** Blame is akin to defensiveness, but it's even more active and destructive. When something goes wrong, many people will search for a scapegoat to assign blame. It's a way to avoid the feeling of being caught in the cross-hairs of potentially tough situations.

**Closed-Mindedness.** Closed-mindedness is potentially the most limiting (and thereby the most destructive) of the four thinking styles. It's when we convince ourselves of our own expertise—that we have nothing more to learn, and therefore don't need to be open to unfamiliar, or uncomfortable, ideas.

## MANAGING YOUR OWN FEAR

Here's something else worth remembering about boxed-in thinking: it's very common! In fact, at some point in our lives, each of us has chosen to stay inside this box of limitations, and at some point in the future, we will all fall into the box again. That's because engaging in these four behaviors (and living inside this box of limitations) provides a sense of safety.

Here's the truth about the box: that sense of safety is an illusion. Remaining boxed-in is about fear—the fear of new ideas that may challenge your comfort. Engaging in the behaviors that make up the box is a form of the *Adversity-Fear-Paralysis Cycle*. That's because as long as you engage in those behaviors, you can't use new ideas to grow and evolve. The hostility that people who are boxed-in sometimes develop towards new ideas is a symptom of *paralysis*.

### FIGURE 10

## Fear

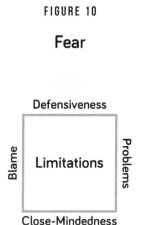

The kind of fear that leads to boxed-in thinking—and keeps people paralyzed within the box of limitations—is especially dangerous in a highly disruptive and rapidly evolving world. It's a prime reason why people get left behind, while those who can break free of the box go on to evolve, adapt, and find the opportunities that so often accompany disruption.

## CASE STUDY: AN ENTIRE COMPANY LEFT BEHIND BECAUSE OF BOXED-IN THINKING

Once a giant in the recording and entertainment industry, Columbia House is an example of an entire company that got left behind because of a culture of boxed-in thinking. The business (originally called the Columbia Record Club) was founded in 1955 by CBS/Columbia Records, with a business model that was novel at the time: the company sold records by mail order. It opened up markets that lacked brick-and-mortar retail music stores, like rural communities. The business pioneered a novel concept in marketing at the time by giving away one free record just for joining the club.

The concept was a success. The business grew rapidly and quickly expanded beyond just the original rural communities. In the early days, Columbia House also kept pace with changing technology in the entertainment industry. Its leaders enhanced their product lines as recording technology evolved from records to cassette tapes to 8-track tapes, and then to CDs. Columbia House also expanded its product line to include movies (VHS tapes and DVDs) as the home entertainment industry expanded. The business peaked in 1994, when Columbia House accounted for 15% of all CD sales and boasted a club membership of 16 million customers (Funding Universe, n.d.).

But the success was not to last. In the late-1990s, Columbia House failed to comprehend the threat (and the opportunity) of an emerging disruption—the Internet. By early 2000, Amazon had entered the mail-order CD business, and Columbia House was floundering. Amazon could offer similar discounts, without the commitment of a CD club subscription. By 2001, Columbia House's market share had declined to less than 8% of CD sales (Funding Universe, n.d.). Businesses like iTunes and Netflix followed. Columbia House filed for bankruptcy in August of 2015 (Wattles, 2015).

## MY TIME AT COLUMBIA HOUSE

I had an inside view into the goings-on at Columbia House because I worked there in the mid-1990s, leading a marketing function, when the company was reaching its peak.

At the time I had a colleague and friend at the company, Linda, who was facing some career struggles that were really about the same internal dynamics that would ultimately doom the company.

Linda had an idea that she was passionate about and desperately wanted to pursue. She believed the Internet was going to have a big impact on the business, and she wanted Columbia House to get involved early. But Linda couldn't get her boss or anyone else at the company to take her seriously. In 1997, after two years of frustration, she left the company. In February of 2000, Columbia House would announce plans to re-tool its business to go online, but by then the efforts would ultimately prove to be too little, too late.

There were a couple of things that made Linda's challenge even harder. She was a woman in a male-dominated culture. She was also young, and a newly-minted MBA in a company lead by "old-timers" who'd been there for decades. Linda simply didn't fit the mold. I didn't either. I also left within a couple of years, and so did virtually all of the forward-thinking new blood the company managed to bring in.

The most difficult part of working at Columbia House was that the company culture was thoroughly hobbled by the fourth wall of *Boxed-In Thinking*: Closed-Mindedness. The company was run by a tight-knit, insular "old-boys' network." They were people who'd been with the company for many years—some for their entire careers—and they were unshakably confident in their own brilliance. Anyone who didn't fit their mold was regarded with skepticism, and any ideas that challenged the status-quo were quickly rejected. They saw the company's record of success as proof-positive of their wisdom.

Columbia House wasn't alone. Many organizations with a long history of past success encounter this challenge. There can be a strong temptation to assume the future will look just like the past—and therefore, to believe the same behaviors that drove past success will also lead to future success. However, as we've discussed, we now live in a highly dynamic and disruptive world; a world that's changing far too quickly to rely on past behaviors. Becoming overly confident in your abilities based on past success is an example of boxed-in thinking. *Out-of-the-Box Thinking* (and a **Thriving Mindset**) means just the opposite: it's about maintaining a certain degree of skepticism and always questioning whether what you've done in the past will be adequate for tomorrow.

Here's the accurate picture about what was going on for Columbia House: the music industry was about to be disrupted, and Columbia House was about to be left behind. The Columbia House business failure is ironic because the company's initial success came from an innovative business concept, music and video subscription clubs. The company had also kept pace with advancing technology and trends in the home entertainment industry. Who was better suited than Columbia House to re-imagine what home entertainment would become? Plus, Columbia House had a foothold in the entertainment industry and a vast customer base that the newcomers lacked.

But just like Kodak, Columbia House suffered from boxed-in thinking—especially with regard to closed-mindedness among senior leadership—and thus, they too fell prey to the *Adversity-Fear-Paralysis Cycle*.

## HOW TO BREAK OUT OF THE BOX

The key to avoiding this *paralysis* of ⌐
recognizing when you are responding to dis⌐
ing in "boxed-in behaviors"—defensiveness, blame,
in terms of problems, and closed-mindedness. Then, inu
tionally exchange the (perceived) safety of the box for the
discomfort of a more courageous approach.

Essentially, it's about taking a specific type of *Courageous Leap*. It means replacing the four walls of the box with
a different behaviors—behaviors that replace the limitations
of the box with empowerment, and that, in turn, allow you
to actively *Trade in the Currency of Ideas.*

### FIGURE 11

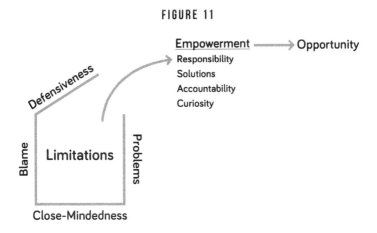

- *Defensiveness* must transform into *Responsibility*: Rather
  than becoming defensive, people who engage in *Out-Of-
  the-Box Thinking* are quick to step forward and take on
  responsibility, even when it's uncomfortable or frightening.
- *The Problem* mindset must transform into a *Solution*
  mindset: Rather than thinking in terms of problems,

Black Friday was just around the corner, which, as the start of the holiday shopping season, is critical in retail. It had already been a tough year for Gap. Company sales had been on the decline since 2014. That's because Gap hadn't kept pace with online shopping trends. Its systems were antiquated and disjointed, and the company couldn't meet consumer expectations for a seamless online/off-line shopping experience, fast order fulfillment, or excellent customer service. This disruption was the perfect recipe for boxed-in thinking that would have trapped the company in a downward spiral of the *Adversity-Fear-Paralysis Cycle*.

But Gap took a very different course. Its leaders seized upon this disruption as a source of opportunity and thus the genesis of a two-year-long wave of innovation that ultimately changed the course of the entire business.

The first priority was responding to the more than 1,200 Fishkill employees who were (at least temporarily) out of work. Gap chose to continue their paychecks, even when there wasn't a job to go to, recognizing that this was an opportunity to galvanize its workforce.

Then came the challenge of managing demand for the upcoming 2016 holiday season. Of course, the company looked to the other North American fulfillment centers—from Gallatin, Tennessee, to Fresno, California—to pick up as much as possible. But leaders also needed to think on the fly and come up with novel solutions. One was a "pop-up" fulfillment center that was constructed in one of the still-standing storage units at Fishkill. Merchandise was lined up on racks so that workers could pick and pack orders by hand, rather than with the normal automated equipment. It took four times as many employees to get the work done, but they got the orders out.

The most important thing Gap did was that they used the disruption caused by the fire to reimagine how its warehouses should operate, not only at Fishkill but across the entire company. Prior to the fire, the company was operating on machinery that had been purchased in the late 1990s. The equipment still had many years of useful life-time left, so it would have been difficult to make a business case for scrapping the equipment. But it had been designed prior to the demand of the Internet shopping era.

After the fire, the company got to start again from a fresh slate. Its decision-makers started rethinking all of their logistics, designed processes that were a better match with customer expectations, and upgraded technology. The rebuilt Fishkill plant also became an incubator for new ideas; the ideas that worked there were rolled out to the entire company.

Not only did Gap survive the fire and rebuild the Fishkill facility, but the firm also reversed a downward trend in the business overall. By the fourth quarter of 2017, the next holiday buying season after the fire, sales were up by 7.9% (Segran, 2018). There were other positive changes too, including an improved product line and better advertising, but the company credits the fire as a major moment of innovation.

Gap's response to the disruption of this warehouse fire is a case study in all of the steps for taking a *Courageous Leap* into *Outside-of-the-Box* thinking. The company faced a very serious disruption at an extremely inopportune time; when sales were declining. Its leaders could have given in to the limitations of the box: **Blamed** the fire for unfavorable business results, become **Defensive,** looked at the devastation of the fire as a **Problem** they couldn't overcome and remained **Closed-Minded** about the need for change at the company.

But Gap took a very different path. By embracing the disruption as what they called a "no excuses moment," leaders were able to find an important opportunity for innovation and growth.

## CHAPTER SUMMARY—PUTTING IT ALL TOGETHER

In this chapter, we discussed developing the ability to *Trade in The Currency of Ideas*, and how that ability is a critical part of *The Thriving Mindset*.

### Some Key Points to Remember

- The *Four Forces of Change* we discussed in Chapter 1—and the *Learning Economy* that has emerged—have created a world where ideas have become an important form of currency. The world is now hungry for individuals with the ability to be creative and innovative.

- Advances in technology have made it easier than ever to bring new ideas to market quickly, and the rewards can be very high.

- People who can bring new ideas to the table, articulate those ideas well, engage with others to refine and evolve those ideas, and ultimately act on those ideas, are at a distinct advantage.

- *Trading in The Currency of Ideas* means cultivating your ability for *Out-of-The-Box Thinking*, rather than engaging in the behaviors of *Boxed-In-Thinking*.

- *Boxed-In-Thinking* happens when fear causes people to engage in self-limiting behaviors like *Defensiveness, Blame, Problem-centric thinking, and Close-Mindedness.*

Breaking out of the box means taking a *Courageous Leap* towards empowering behaviors.

## Key Questions to Think About

1. What's an example of someone who is really good at *Trading in The Currency of Ideas*? This might be an individual, a group, or maybe an entire organization.
2. When have you observed someone engage in *Boxed-In Thinking*? It might have been an individual, a team, or maybe even an entire organization.
3. What was causing them to become boxed-in?
4. What was something they could have done to break out of the box?
5. When have you seen someone use their ability for *Out-Of-the-Box Thinking* to help them *Trade in The Currency of Ideas*?

CHAPTER SEVEN

# BUILDING A PRACTICE
# OF SELF-CARE

Practicing self-care is a critical part of cultivating *The Thriving Mindset*. But self-care is also something that's often overlooked and misunderstood. One of my most important self-care practices is running. In fact, becoming a runner is how I overcame the weight problem that plagued me in my early life. I began running during the summer of my sophomore year in college. Over the next several years, the pounds came off, and, most importantly, I discovered that I absolutely love running—that is, when I'm not being tormented by a maniacal high school soccer coach!

Since then, during the most challenging times, I have turned to running and other endurance sports as a source of stress release and solace. As I began to run more seriously after college, I discovered that I also loved racing, and ultimately added swimming and cycling to my regime so that I could compete in triathlons.

## THE MYTH ABOUT WHAT SELF-CARE LOOKS LIKE

This picture was taken during a triathlon in which I competed in during the mid-1990s. This particular race was what's called a "Half-Ironman" and is composed of a 1.2-mile swim, a 56-mile bike ride, and a 13.1-mile run. It's also called an "Ironman 70.3" because you complete a total distance of 70.3 miles under your own power.

### FIGURE 12

### THE FORMER "FAT KID" COMPETING IN A TRIATHLON

(PHOTO CREDIT: PICTURE COURTESY OF GERRY VALENTINE)

I remember when this picture was taken. I'd just completed the swim portion of the race, and we were running to hop on our bicycles. It's a remarkable picture to look back on for a few reasons. First, it's a far cry from my days as the "fat kid" on the soccer team. I am always stunned that I was able to transition my body into this level of athletic condition.

Second, I remember what was on my mind. Although I was in what would turn out to be the peak athletic condition of my life, this wasn't a moment of celebration and joy. Instead, I was thinking about my athletic shortcomings. There were a couple of guys in front of me, people I knew from training and from other races, and I was unhappy with myself because I wasn't fast enough to keep up with them. I wasn't able to enjoy my accomplishments.

But the most important thing about this picture is the myth that's hidden behind it: The myth of what self-care is and what it looks like. When this picture was taken, I was training as much as 12 to 15 hours a week. I looked extremely strong and healthy, like someone who takes excellent care of himself. But this is not a picture of a man practicing self-care.

In addition to all of my triathlon training, I was also putting in 60 to 70-hour work weeks in the office at an extremely high-stress job. If you do the math, you'll see that, between working and working out, there wasn't room for much else other than eating and sleeping. I had virtually no social life, very few friendships, and no family life to speak of in those years. I was stressed out all the time at work, and I was using extreme exercise as a solution to feeling isolated, lonely, and unhappy. It wouldn't be long before the reality that's hidden behind this picture started to hit me.

There was one piece of incredibly good fortune during those years. I met the man who would ultimately become the love of my life and my husband, Daniel Blausey. Not surprisingly, he was another endurance runner, and he ultimately took up triathlons and Ironman competitions too. But he took a much more balanced and healthy approach to his athletics than I did; he is also a much better athlete than I am.

Daniel was the first person to observe that I was burning myself out. I would put in the hours to train, and I'd show up to races, but it was often clear that I didn't want to be there. It wasn't long before injuries started to appear, simply because I was pushing myself and my body too far. In those days, I would have told you that I put in just as much dedication in the office as I did in my training. I was working for high-profile companies. I thrived on the competition and pressure (or so I told myself). I was committed to moving up the corporate ladder, and I maintained a rock-solid façade at work. I was successful, and the salary was great. However, in retrospect, I now also know that I wasn't bringing my "A-game" to the office either. Underneath my impenetrable façade, the pressure and isolation were getting to me, and there were many times when I was simply too burnt-out to be my best-self for the company or for the people I was leading.

I needed to better practice self-care in order to be at my best.

## WHY HIGH-PERFORMERS OFTEN FALL PREY TO POOR SELF-CARE

One word I would have used to describe myself at the time is "driven," and I wanted to be seen as a high-performer in all aspects of my life. One important lesson I've learned since is that driven, high-performer types are very likely to fall prey to poor self-care practices. And we do it at our own peril.

Here's why that happens and why it's so dangerous.

**FIGURE 13**

**HIGH-PERFORMERS & SELF CARE**

People who fall into the driven, high-achiever personality type tend to see the road in front of them as a kind of ladder. Each step takes them higher toward "achievement." They often don't look back on what they've accomplished, only ahead to what comes next. And very often, with every rung they climb towards achievement, there's an inverted image that's outside of the person's awareness: the steps down into increasingly poor self-care.

**FIGURE 14**

**HIGH-PERFORMERS & SELF CARE**

As high-achievers push themselves toward higher and higher goals, they tend to sacrifice more and more on the self-care front. It can start slowly—giving up an hour or two of sleep to finish that big project, for example, which later turns into always sleeping less so you can get into the office earlier or stay later. This ultimately becomes a habit of giving up time for exercise, or family, or something else, and the cycle continues.

When the delta between achievement and self-care reaches a certain critical point, burnout occurs.

### FIGURE 15

### HIGH-PERFORMERS & SELF CARE

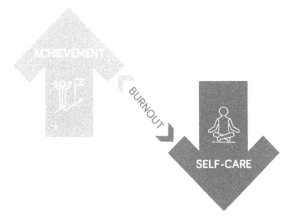

Different people have different amounts of tolerance before they reach burnout, but everyone has a breaking point. You can also think of the increasing delta between achievement and practicing self-care as analogous to the *Adversity-Fear-Paralysis Cycle.* Many high-performers report a reluctance to back off and take better care of themselves for *fear* of missing an opportunity. It's a fear I understand. During my most intense corporate and triathlon days,

I certainly would have been reluctant to—or more accurately, afraid to—back off on any front. But it's a fear that (if not addressed productively) ultimately leads to *paralysis* because when burnout does occur (whatever form that burnout may take), it will likely cost you far more.

## ESTABLISHING A PRACTICE OF INTENTIONAL SELF-CARE

The answer to mitigating the risk of burnout is to establish a practice of what I call *"Intentional Self-Care"*. *A Practice of Intentional Self-Care* is actually ideally suited to high-performing individuals because it taps into the natural tenacity and dedication and focuses that energy on establishing effective care of the self, all for the purpose of supporting long-term success and the long-term ability to thrive.

The first step in establishing a *Practice of Intentional Self-Care* is understanding and accepting that the "self" is both important and critical. Put simply, you cannot perform your best—in whatever way may be important to you—if you don't take proper care of yourself.

Next, rather than thinking about self-care as a single, "check-the-box" step, I recommend that people consider practicing self-care along three dimensions—Physical Health, Emotional Health, and Social Health.

**Physical Health.** This is about how well you take care of your body. It includes things like getting regular exercise and enough sleep, having regular physicals and dental check-ups, and following through on any known health issues. It's about making sure that your physical self is in the best shape so that you can be at you best when faced with life's demands.

FIGURE 16

A PRACTICE OF INTENTIONAL SELF-CARE

**Social Health.** Humans are inherently social creatures. In fact, according to studies quoted in WebMD, chronic loneliness brings morbidity and mortality risks that rival those of smoking and obesity (Tate, 2018). Often when people strive for achievement, they may let go of social relationships with family and friends. As we will discuss in Chapter 11 (*Cultivating Social Capital*), social connections are critical for providing us with the insight and agency necessary to thrive in challenging times. However, there's another equally important perspective related to social health, and that is that it's a critical part of self-care.

**Emotional Health.** Our emotional health is linked to our physical health and our social health, but it also goes further. Emotional health is also about our sense of fulfillment, our ability to relax and rejuvenate, connection with community, and for some, religious and/or spiritual beliefs. In fact, protecting emotional health is even more important in our modern-day, disruptive world. Increasing amounts of research have linked a very specific and prevalent part of our modern lifestyle—social media use (e.g., the *Mass Interconnectivity Force of Change* we spoke about in Chapter 1)—with increased rates of anxiety and depression (Reed, 2020).

For me, establishing a *Practice of Intentional Self-Care* meant achieving much more balance and using my participation in endurance sports—something I really enjoy—in a healthier way. The first thing was turning up the focus on my social health. I had to find more opportunities to cultivate fulfilling and supportive relationships. Meeting my future husband and creating a more balanced and fulfilling life together was one very important part of that.

Another part was bringing my professional life into better balance with my needs. Despite the challenges of life in the corporate world, I enjoyed that part of my career. I also realized I could approach my career with more of a sense of abundance and appreciation—as something I was very grateful to have—and not just as gut-wrenching competition. That shift made more space for cultivating all aspects of *Practicing Intentional Self-Care*, and it's a shift that can benefit many high-achievers.

When I transitioned from my corporate career into running my own business, the shift and balance became even more important. As any business owner will tell you, your business permeates your entire life, and there can be a tendency to conflate your business life and your personal life. Sometimes that's great, because it can be an expression of your passion about your business. However, that passion also comes with the need to maintain balance. Just as was once the case with endurance sports, I now need to be mindful of maintaining balance and using the passion for my business in a healthy way—one that's aligned with a *Practice of Intentional Self-Care*.

There is one more important thing to remember about practicing self-care: it's an ongoing process, not a one-time event. As you move through life, your career, and changes in your circumstance, you will need to continually come back to these three pillars to make sure you stay in balance. You will need to ensure that your drive to achieve isn't ultimately setting you up for burnout.

## CHAPTER SUMMARY—PUTTING IT ALL TOGETHER

In this chapter, we discussed one often overlooked part of cultivating a *Thriving Mindset*: building a *Practice of Self-Care*.

### Some Key Points to Remember

- Just as with the other topics I've discussed, a *Practice of Self-Care* better enables you to take *Courageous Leaps* at times of disruption. People who neglect self-care will find themselves more limited because they are at risk of burning-out at critical moments.
- Achievement-oriented, "high-performers," are especially vulnerable to poor self-care. That's because they often get into the habit of making small sacrifices of their self-care for the sake of achievement. Over time, the sacrifices add-up and ultimately lead to burnout.
- The solution is to implement a *Practice of Intentional Self-Care*, which includes three building blocks:
  - **Physical Health:** Attending to your physical needs like sleep, proper nutrition, exercise, and medical care.
  - **Social Health:** Dedicating the time to building supportive friendships and family relationships.

Cultivating social health also has an added benefit in that it leads to increased *Social Capital*, which we will discuss in Chapter 11.

○ **Emotional Health:** This is about our sense of fulfillment, our ability to relax and rejuvenate, connection with community, and for some, religious and/or spiritual beliefs. Protecting emotional health is even more important in our modern-day, hyper-connected world because high usage of technologies like social media have been shown to have a detrimental effect on emotional health.

## Key Questions to Think About

1. What self-care practices do you engage in each day?
2. Have there been times when you experienced "burnout"? If so, what were those times like?
3. Are you paying adequate attention to all three building blocks of self-care—physical health, social health, and emotional health—or are you falling short in some areas?
4. What is at least one additional *Intentional Self-Care Practice* you could add to your daily routine? It doesn't necessarily need to be big. Small things, like taking a walk around the block, can have a big impact when done consistently.

CHAPTER EIGHT

# THRIVING THROUGH FAILURE

One question I like to ask new clients is: when was a time you had a significant failure, and how did you handle it? The answer can reveal a lot about the person's ability to thrive during times of disruption. That's because failure is a necessary tool for growth. Our mindset about failure and our ability to handle disruption can determine whether we take *Courageous Leaps* or get trapped in *the Adversity-Fear-Paralysis Cycle*. Ultimately, cultivating a productive mindset about failure is a fundamental part of cultivating **The Thriving Mindset**.

Most of the time, when people ask about *Thriving Through Failure*, they mean: How do I survive failure? It's the wrong question and perspective on failure. The more productive way of looking at failure is as a source of learning, innovation, and growth. That means the correct question to ask about *Thriving Through Failure* is: How can I *use failure as a means to thrive*?

Sometimes the things that initially seem like failures are really pathways to opportunity and innovation. Viagra®, the "little blue pill" that treats male erectile dysfunction, is one example. Viagra is one of the world's best-known prescription products, but it is actually the result of a failure. The active ingredient in Viagra (Sildenafil) was originally developed by Pfizer Pharmaceuticals as a treatment for hypertension (high blood pressure) and angina pectoris (chest pain due to heart disease). During clinical trials, researchers noticed that the medication had an unusual side effect: it caused male study participants to have an erection. Sildenafil ultimately wasn't a particularly effective treatment for hypertension and angina—essentially a clinical failure—but the medication was successful at inducing erections.

Leaders at Pfizer realized there was an unmet medical need in treating erectile dysfunction, and an unexpected business opportunity, in an untapped market, arose. The medication was re-branded as Viagra, and it became the first FDA approved oral treatment for erectile dysfunction. Viagra became a highly recognized brand (with as much brand name recognition as Coke or Nike) and an enormous business success. The product would achieve more than $2 billion in sales the year it was first launched (2008), which was the fastest initial sales growth for any prescription product at the time (WebMD, 2020). In addition, Viagra played a pivotal role in de-stigmatizing erectile dysfunction, a condition that affects an estimated 30 million men in the United States, allowing sufferers to more easily have conversations with their healthcare providers (WebMD, 2020). Because erectile dysfunctions can also be an indicator of more serious underlying medical conditions—like hypertension, high cholesterol, and diabetes—this de-stigmatization was incredibly important to many men's overall wellness and self-care. All of that from a product "failure."

Not all failures result in an immediate success like Viagra. But any substantial success is virtually always preceded by failure, and typically by many failures. When we think of humanity's most significant achievements—things like powered flight, space travel, electricity, and the combustion engine—they were all preceded by many failures. Successes eventually happened because of people who understood how to use their failures as a means to improve their ideas, to find opportunity, and to innovate. They understood this essential part of *The Thriving Mindset*.

The problem is that most people experience failure as a crushing defeat, rather than as an opportunity for learning and innovation. When you experience failure as a defeat, it's impossible to leverage the failure as an opportunity for a *Courageous Leap*.

## THE STORIES WE TELL OURSELVES

Perhaps the biggest determinant of whether people are defeated by a failure, or whether they can leverage failure into opportunity, is the story they tell themselves about the experience of failure. That's because stories are powerful tools for shaping the reality we experience. Sometimes, when we change the stories we tell ourselves, we can create a new, more productive reality.

When I was very young, a holiday ritual in our home was to wait until Christmas Eve to put up our Christmas tree. My mother said this was for good luck. In the days and weeks leading up to Christmas, we'd walk through the neighborhood, admire other trees, and carefully plan what ours would look like that year. My brother's and my excitement would grow as we counted the days until we'd get our tree.

On Christmas Eve, we'd wait for my mother to return from work (which was typically quite late). We'd make the special trip to get the tree, and we'd spend the evening decorating, all while hurrying to make sure we got the tree up before Santa arrived. The ritual made Christmas Eve almost as exciting as Christmas morning. It became a very special day, at a time when we didn't have many special days.

But there is a very different version of the story, one that my mother didn't share with me until many years later. The reason we always got the tree on Christmas Eve was because money was tight, and it was extremely difficult for her to afford a Christmas tree at all. Buying a tree on Christmas Eve meant that she could haggle and get one very cheap. The few trees that were left were typically the ones no one else wanted. The sellers had the option of selling a bedraggled tree to my mother or throwing it away in a few hours.

As kids, we didn't know any of that. My mother used the power of a story—that it was good luck to put the tree up on Christmas Eve—to brighten something that could have been yet another failure. Consequently, the pain and embarrassment of how much we were struggling financially were changed into a much-needed positive experience during the holiday season.

## CHOOSING THE STORY OF EMPOWERMENT AND LEARNING

I've used the Christmas tree story as an example many times over the years—in a business context, in leadership situations, and with my executive coaching clients—because it's an excellent example of how the story we choose to tell in a given situation can dramatically impact how we experience that situation. In most cases, we have the power to choose which version of a story we tell and edit those stories so that they empower us.

For example, we could talk about Viagra as a story about a failed cardiovascular medication or as a story about a revolutionary prescription product. The latter version of the story is about a breakthrough that addressed an unmet medical need, removed stigma, and allowed doctors to identify serious co-existing medical conditions that otherwise might not have been diagnosed. The Christmas tree story could be about financial struggle and deprivation, or it could be about a mother creating a memorable and special experience for her children. It's all about which story you choose.

Most people who've had a significant failure choose a negative version of the story. For example, on any given month, I meet people who will tell me stories like:

- *"My department failed on yet another high-visibility project."*
- *"I got fired because I couldn't cut it at that job."*
- *"I was passed over again for the promotion because I'm not part of the 'in crowd' at my company."*

Like a lot of failure stories, all these examples have a few elements in common: they are static and without opportunity for change, they lack learning and insight, and most importantly, they operate from a place of passivity and disempowerment. *Thriving Through Failure* is often about choosing a different story—a story that puts you in an active role that speaks to empowerment, and that includes the ability to learn, evolve, and change.

Here are examples of some of the more productive stories I've encouraged people to select:

- *"My department needs to become better at executing high-profile projects."*
- *"I need to do some critical introspection about the job I just lost. I need to understand what went wrong and what I could have done differently."*
- *"I need to get a better handle on how I'm seen in my organization. I've been passed over for a few promotions, and I wonder if it's about how I'm perceived."*

## CHANGING TO A MINDSET OF EXPERIMENTATION, LEARNING, AND ADAPTATION

*Thriving Through Failure* is also changing your mindset. Most people operate with a fixed and binary mindset. They see themselves succeeding or failing, they see things as right or wrong, and they look at their abilities as fixed: they can do something, or they cannot. That kind of rigidity puts people at risk for falling into the *Adversity-Fear-Paralysis Cycle*.

The most effective mindset for thriving is far more nuanced. It's about seeing everything we do as an experiment that allows for continuous learning and adaptation. Growth isn't possible without occasional failure. In fact, the only people who don't fail are the ones who don't stretch themselves and thus never grow. The key is to see failure as part of experimentation and to locate the important lessons in the failure. When everything is seen as an experiment, and when the goal is learning and adaptation, nothing can be a crushing failure.

This not-so-subtle *Thriving Mindset* shift allows people to more easily create the aforementioned stories of empowerment that lead to growth.

## SELF-CARE AND SOCIAL CAPITAL DURING TIMES OF FAILURE

In the previous chapter, we discussed an important part of thriving: Self-Care. We'll be discussing the importance of *Social Capital*—the people we bring into our circle—in the chapters ahead. Both *Self-Care* and *Social Capital* are especially important when it comes to creating the mindset necessary to *Thrive Through Failure*.

Even in the best of circumstances, failure can be a very difficult experience. Even when we create stories of empowerment, and when we adjust our mindset toward experimentation and learning, failure can still eat at our confidence and self-esteem. That's when it's important to lean on our self-care practices and to devote more time to a *Practice of Intentional Self-Care*.

The times when we're working through failure are also the times to be leveraging *Social Capital* (which we'll be discussing in Chapter 10) and making sure we're surrounding ourselves with the right people. We need people who can help us choose stories of empowerment, help us stay in the experimentation and continuous improvement mindset, and help us identify and learn the right lessons; such that we can thrive as a result of the failure.

## CHAPTER SUMMARY—PUTTING IT ALL TOGETHER

In this chapter, we discussed why our mindset about failure and our ability to handle failure could determine whether we take *Courageous Leaps* or get trapped in the *Adversity-Fear-Paralysis Cycle.* Learning to handle failure productively is a fundamental part of *The Thriving Mindset.*

### Some Key Points to Remember

- Most people think about how to survive failure; that's the wrong perspective. Always look at failure as a source of learning, innovation, and growth.
- The stories we choose to tell ourselves about our failures help determine how well we can handle failure. Always choose stories of empowerment, experimentation, and learning.
- Taking appropriate care of ourselves (cultivating a *Practice of Self-Care*) and surrounding ourselves with the right people (cultivating *Social Capital*) are critical for *Thriving Through Failure.*

### Key Questions to Think About

1. When was a time when you had a significant failure?
2. At the time, what was your reaction to the failure—did you see it as a crushing experience or a learning opportunity?
3. What is one thing you can do to help yourself experience future failures as experiments—opportunities for learning and growth?

4. How might you use a past failure to set you up for a future *Courageous Leap*?
5. How might you exercise *Intentional Self-Care* to help you put failure in the right perspective?
6. Who in your circle of contacts—friends, mentors, bosses, colleagues, etc.—can help you take an "experimentation", "lessons learned", and "opportunity for growth" perspective on failure?

CHAPTER NINE

# UNDERSTANDING WEALTH AND CREATING FINANCIAL HEALTH

There's an old saying that "money won't make you happy." That's true, but there's something else that people don't talk about enough: *Not having enough* **wealth** *will make you very* <u>*unhappy*</u>. If you doubt that, just ask anyone who (like me) has ever lived in poverty. That's because—although money alone won't make you happy—wealth provides an important foundation for thriving, especially at times of disruption. Wealth provides access to opportunity and a stable safety net when facing uncertainty. Those two things combined—access to opportunity and a stable safety net—are often the foundation for making *Courageous Leaps.*

People generally think about wealth in terms of money or being "rich." Having a sufficient amount of money is an important part of wealth, but there is more than just money to the kind of wealth that's necessary for thriving through disruptive times. The "wealth" that I'm referring to includes three components—three specific things that will support you through adversity and disruption: *Financial Health, Intellectual Capital*, and *Social Capital*.

FIGURE 17

THE THREE TYPES OF WEALTH

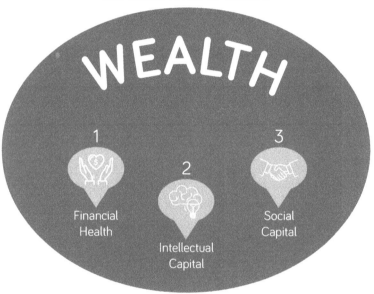

*Financial Health* isn't about making a high salary or having a specific amount of money in the bank. It's about having adequate access to the financial resources necessary to thrive. *Financial Health* is also about attitudes and practices around money and about having an effective understanding of money (e.g., financial literacy.) *Intellectual Capital* is about how you cultivate your knowledge base and how you utilize your knowledge. *Social Capital* is about the connections you build and how you utilize those connections to unlock opportunity. In this chapter, we're going to examine the *Financial Health* component of wealth. In the next two chapters, we will delve into *Intellectual Capital* and *Social Capital*, respectively.

## A LESSON IN FINANCIAL HEALTH

I started learning about *Financial Health*—or more accurately, *lack* of *Financial Health*—soon after I graduated from Cornell University in 1985. I had earned a Bachelor of Science Degree in Electrical Engineering, with a concentration in computer hardware and software. It was an extremely marketable degree, which was a big part of my reason for selecting that field of study. Three months before graduation, I landed my first job offer with a substantial starting annual salary—I was ecstatic! It was more money than my family had ever made. All the work and expense of college seemed like a huge success, and I was sure this was that first step into a comfortable middle-class life.

I'd also made a promise to myself midway through college: If I could handle the course work, graduate on time, and land a good-paying job, I would reward myself with a new car after graduation. I'd always watched much wealthier friends drive fancy new cars their parents had purchased for them. In college, I managed to buy a 10-year-old rust-bucket. I'd paid about $1,000 for it, but everyone thought I'd overpaid—that's how bad the car was. I wanted to finally have a car that could be a source of pride. Once the job offer was finalized, I rewarded myself. I bought a brand new, graphite black, 1986 Volkswagen Scirocco. The down payment consumed much of the money I'd saved in my summer internships during college, but that was okay. After all, I was making a huge salary (at least in my mind) and could soon replenish my savings. It was an amazing feeling when I drove that car off the lot—to have worked so hard, to have succeeded, to have beaten the odds in so many ways, and to now have earned the reward I'd wanted so much.

But the story didn't end when I drove off the car lot. The job I'd landed turned out to be a nightmare. It was supposed to be a management training program, with a very well-known company, but the job wasn't what the company had represented. There was very little "management training", and this job wasn't going to give me the experience I needed to start my career. I hated every moment at work, and I disliked the isolated area where I was living. Plus, I was commuting more than 30 miles each way daily, because the company was in an even more remote area. It was a deeply depressing start to my career and an enormous disappointment when compared to what I'd anticipated. That new car provided very little solace.

As time went on, I learned more about the expectations of the business world, and I soon realized that my career aspirations required an MBA. Fortunately for me, my undergraduate degree in engineering was also attractive to business schools. I started applying to graduate schools within the first six months on the job, and was accepted into the MBA program at the New York University Stern School of Management. It was a top-ranked MBA program, and they'd also offered me a generous scholarship.

But there was a serious problem: the money I owed on that new car. Everything else could be put on hold, and I was content to be a "poor" student again, but I couldn't afford the car payments without that high-paying job I hated so much.

I also owed significantly more on the car than it was now worth in resale. That's because of something I didn't have the financial acumen to understand at the time: new cars depreciate substantially immediately after purchase, and (unless you make a significant down-payment), you can quickly find yourself "upside-down" in an auto loan. It seemed like I had only two (very undesirable) options: 1) Let the incredible opportunity of getting a top-ranked MBA slip away (along with the scholarship money), so I could stay at a terrible job, and pay for a car I no longer wanted, or 2) Default on my car loan, and ruin my credit, endangering the student loans I'd also need for business school.

I was lucky: I found another solution. I was able to take out an additional student loan, which, when combined with most of the money I'd managed to save in my first year of work, gave me just enough to pay off the extra money I owed on the car. I was back to square one financially. Once again, I had almost no savings, but I was able to start business school. I made the money back quickly because my total compensation upon graduation was more than double what I'd been making before. But it was a close call and an important lesson about how just one bad financial decision (one that leads to poor *Financial Health*) can cost you a critical opportunity.

## DECISIONS OF DESPERATION VS. COURAGEOUS LEAPS

I've coined a term for what almost happened to me in those early years after college: a *"decision of desperation."* That's what happens when, rather than having the opportunity to make a *Courageous Leap*, you are forced into making suboptimal, short-term decisions just to survive. It's when financial (or sometimes other circumstances) cause you to lose access to opportunity. I had a once-in-a-lifetime opportunity of admission to a top-notch business school and the scholarship money to make it a reality. But being in poor *Financial Health* almost forced me into a *decision of desperation*: staying in an awful job and giving up the admission offer (and the scholarship money) because of the debt hanging over my head. Creating good *Financial Health* (the financial resources necessary to unlock opportunity and a healthy relationship with money) is what protects you from being forced into those *decisions of desperation* and enables you to make *Courageous Leaps*.

## THERE'S AN EPIDEMIC OF POOR FINANCIAL HEALTH

I wasn't alone in my post-college decision that led to poor *Financial Health*. In fact, there's an epidemic of poor *Financial Health* among Americans of all ages. An estimated 69% of U.S. adults have less than $1,000 in savings, and 34% have no savings at all (Backman, 2017). In fact, 78% of U.S. workers live paycheck to paycheck (Friedman, 2019). According to the Federal Reserve's 2017 Report on the Economic Well-Being of U.S. Households, 44% of Americans don't have enough cash on hand to cover a $400 unexpected expense (The Federal Reserve, 2017). The average out-of-pocket expense for an emergency room visit is over $1,300, so almost half of Americans are just one accident away from a significant bill they can't pay (Alltucker, 2019), and potential financial disaster. Ironically, more people than ever are in exactly the same position I was when trying to sell my car after college (Jones, 2018). Approximately one-third of new car sales are made to people who have "negative equity" on their trade-in vehicle—meaning, they were upside-down on their car loan (Jones, 2018).

Living under financial stress, from paycheck to paycheck with very little in savings and expensive debt, takes a significant toll. That type of financial ill-health puts people at risk of being forced into *decisions of desperation*, prevents people from accessing opportunity and *Courageous Leaps*, and causes people to get stuck in the *Adversity-Fear-Paralysis Cycle*. For example, if you only have a few months of emergency savings (or perhaps no emergency savings at all), it's very difficult to do things like invest in more education that will payout in the long run, pursue a high-risk / high-reward business idea, stand up to an abusive boss, or speak up if you witness improper or illegal behavior at work. Instead, you're much more likely to make a *decision of desperation*: to just keep your head down, not rock the boat, give up on an opportunity, or look the other way in the face of wrongdoing.

We are not all going to become rich. But we can all improve our *Financial Health* and, in turn, give ourselves better access to the opportunities that good *Financial Health* brings.

## THE FOUR ROOT CAUSES OF POOR FINANCIAL HEALTH

For most people, there are four things at the root of poor *Financial Health*: conflating self-worth with net-worth, financial shame, poor financial literacy, and confusing salary with wealth.

1. **Conflating net-worth with self-worth:**
   Our society often conflates the idea of net-worth with self-worth. We instinctively assume that people who are wealthy are better. They are often seen as more capable, more intelligent, and harder working (Parker, 2012). By extension, we also believe that those who are not wealthy are less intelligent, less capable, and have not worked hard enough.

   In reality, the single most important thing anyone can do to become wealthy isn't about capability, working hard, or intelligence. It's about picking the right parents. Statistically, 45% of the wealthiest Americans inherited their wealth (Sawhill and Rodrigue, 2015). And, circumstances of birth are playing an increasingly important role in financial wealth outcomes later in life as upward mobility rates in the U.S. have declined. For example, a child born in 1940 had a 90% chance of earning a better living than his parents in his lifetime (Reeves and Krause, 2018). However, a child born in 1980 has only a 50% chance of faring better than his parents (Reeves and Krause, 2018). In addition, some groups (like African Americans) have faced historical exclusion from tools for building wealth (and sometimes legally mandated exclusion), and the results of that exclusion are dramatic. An African American boy born into poverty (as I once was) has only an 8% chance of reaching the upper middle class or higher in adulthood (Bradger, 2018).

   Of course, all people need to take responsibility for making good decisions that lead to good *Financial Health*. But it's also important to recognize the factors that lead to high wealth and how much is due simply to an accident of birth. Conflating net-worth with self-worth is destructive and actually contributes to poor *Financial Health*. That's what causes people to make poor financial decisions (often getting themselves into unnecessary debt) in an effort to create an appearance of wealth.

2. **Financial shame:**
   The reason that conflating net-worth with self-worth is so destructive is that it almost always leads to financial shame, and shame is unhealthy. Psychologist and researcher Dr. Brené Brown defines shame as an "intensely painful feeling or experience of believing that we are flawed and therefore unworthy..." I believe Dr. Brown's definition applies to wealth and money as well. I have found that, when people believe that their net worth is indicative of their self-worth, but they haven't amassed as much money as they would like, they often carry shame about money, along with a belief that they are somehow flawed or unworthy.

   The financial shame leads to unhealthy actions around money. It causes people to stop talking about money and their financial situation, and thus cuts people off from the resources they need to become financially healthy, often at the times when they need those resources the most. Roughly 76 million Americans report that they are financially struggling or just getting by—that's almost a third of the population (Tami Luhby, 2016). But only about 25% of those in distress say that they're willing to discuss the situation with anyone else. In fact, Americans are almost twice as likely to share that they're having a marital or relationship issue as they are to share that they're having problems with credit card debt (Lending

Club & Harris Poll, 2018). It's another example of getting trapped in the *Adversity-Fear-Paralysis Cycle*: the adversity of financial struggle triggers fear, conflating net-worth with self-worth causes shame, and shame becomes *paralysis* because it prevents people from discussing their problems and (taking the *Courageous Leap* of) getting the help they need to build *Financial Health*.

I've seen this issue first-hand in my executive coaching practice when I've worked with very successful professionals who are comfortable discussing sensitive business and personal issues, but are reluctant to talk about serious personal financial problems—financial problems that were having a significant impact on their careers. I've also experienced my own financial shame. I was extremely embarrassed when I realized how bad a decision that first car had been, and I didn't want to tell anyone about the financial problems I'd created for myself. But it was precisely the time I would have benefitted the most from reaching out for help.

3. **A lack of financial literacy:**
Most people don't intentionally make poor financial decisions or want to be financially unhealthy. Most people aren't actually irresponsible. Much of the epidemic of poor *Financial Health* is because of poor financial literacy. Two-thirds of Americans can't pass a basic financial literacy test; a test that includes questions like, "If you have $100 in a savings account earning 2% interest a year, after five years, would you have more than $102?" (FINR Investor Education Foundation, 2018) Financial literacy skills also include understanding how to build good credit, how to make good purchasing decisions and use credit productively, and how to establish long-term

financial plans that are aligned with our best interests and will allow us to thrive.

There's also a catch-22 with financial literacy: like wealth, your baseline financial literacy is highly correlated to your parents' wealth. People who were born into affluent (financially healthy) families tend to be far more financially literate because they have access to family members who pass on their knowledge around financial literacy. This access enables them to further increase their wealth and to become even more financially healthy. Most people in my family before my generation had very little access to financial wealth and very little access to financial literacy—so they had very little financial literacy to pass on to me. The same is true for most African Americans, most Latinos, and most white Americans born into low-income families.

4) **Confusing salary with wealth:**

There was another mistake that I made out of college: I'd confused a high salary with wealth. This, too, is a mistake that many people make, and it can be disastrous for *Financial Health*. A salary is something you earn as a result of your work. But a salary can be erratic, unpredictable, and outside of your control. Business downturns or other life events can cause a high salary to drop to zero, like how my life circumstances caused me to leave a high-salary job.

Wealth is different. It's something you own (your assets) and, when managed correctly, something that grows at a predictable rate over time. The assets that make up wealth typically include savings, investments, and equity in your home. It's also important to keep your focus on "net wealth" rather than gross wealth—meaning that your wealth is really total assets minus liabilities like the amount owed on auto loans, credit cards, and other loans. In fact, some economists estimate that half of Americans have "negative net wealth," meaning that their total debts exceed their assets (Steverman, 2019). For example, if you have $1,000 in a savings account, $4,500 in retirement savings, and $6,000 in credit card debt, you actually have a net wealth of _negative_ $500. That doesn't put you in a good position for making _Courageous Leaps_. In my case, despite a high-paying job immediately after college, I had negative net wealth.

When people make the mistake of confusing salary with wealth, it can cause them to believe they're in a better financial position than they really are, and thus make spending decisions that lead to poor _Financial Health._

## A TURNAROUND STORY IN CULTIVATING FINANCIAL HEALTH

There are five key steps for cultivating the _Financial Health_ that will maximize your ability to take _Courageous Leaps_, and thereby thrive at times of disruption:

1) Let go of financial shame.
2) Face your truth about money and the truth about money in your life.
3) Set specific goals and plans around your truth about money.
4) Cultivate your financial literacy.
5) Commit to a long-term practice of _Financial Health_ check-ups.

Here is a real-life story about how those five steps came into play at an important time. I once worked with Ed, a senior executive who felt trapped. He quickly discovered the root cause of his discomfort: he was in very poor *Financial Health*. Although he was making a very good six-figure salary, he was living well beyond his means. Ed's spouse did not work, but they had a very expensive mortgage in an upscale community. They had also amassed significant debt from discretionary spending—like expensive furniture, cars, and home improvements. He would also soon need to pay college tuition for two teenage children. Ed was under a great deal of stress, and the stress was starting to impact many areas of his life—his job performance was suffering, he was irritable at home, and his physical health was beginning to be impacted.

1.  **Letting go of financial shame:**
    Ed carried a great deal of shame about the situation he had created, and our first step was letting go of that shame. He'd constructed an internal story that all of his professional peers were outpacing him financially, so a lot of the family spending was to keep up appearances. In truth, he didn't know anyone else's situation—they could easily have been just as financially strapped. More importantly, the comparison didn't matter—whatever his peer's financial situation might have been, that had no bearing on his truth about money.

    Instead of comparisons, we refocused on his top three major life goals, which were providing for his children's education, someday transitioning to a different career (which would require savings), and taking better care of his health and family relationships.

2. **Face your truth about money, and the truth about money in your life:**

   Comparing his financial situation to his goals revealed an important truth about money in Ed's life. There was a significant gap between the family's goals and their financial reality. Although the family had some savings, the savings weren't anywhere near sufficient to meet their goals. The truth about money in Ed's life was that there was a serous misalignment between his financial reality and his family's goals.

3. **Set specific goals and plans around your truth about money:**

   The truth gave Ed and his family the foundation (and the courage) to make some significant lifestyle adjustments. The family downsized their home, sold one car, and adopted a more frugal lifestyle. It turned out that the high-end appearance they were struggling to keep up wasn't high on anyone's priority list. His spouse also returned to work so the family could increase savings.

4. **Cultivate your financial literacy:**

   Ed and his spouse also recognized that they needed to increase their financial literacy. The fact that they didn't have a great understanding of money was a fundamental part of why they got into trouble in the first place, and they'd need sound advice to meet their future goals. They found a financial advisor who seemed to understand their situation, and one with whom they were comfortable working.

5. **Commit to a long-term practice of Financial Health check-ups:**

   The impact turned out to be much broader than just the family's financial life. Ed's spouse actually enjoyed returning to work. She valued the satisfaction that came from doing more to contribute to the family's well-being. Ed's stress level declined, and his work performance improved. And, perhaps most of all, Ed and his spouse ultimately valued the lesson they were able to pass on to their children at an early age—a lesson about the importance of facing financial truth and the dangers of poor financial health.

## CHAPTER SUMMARY—PUTTING IT ALL TOGETHER

In this chapter, we started discussing the concept of *Wealth* and why cultivating *Wealth* is an important part of building a ***Thriving Mindset***.

### Some Key Points to Remember

- *Wealth* isn't about making a high salary or being "rich." *Wealth* provides access to opportunity and a stable safety net when facing uncertainty. Wealth gives people the opportunity to make *Courageous Leaps*. When people don't have sufficient wealth, they can be forced into "*decisions of desperation*"—often just to survive.
- The three components that make up *Wealth* are: *Financial Health, Social Capital, and Intellectual Capital*. This chapter covered *Financial Health*. *Social Capital* and *Intellectual Capital* are covered in Chapters 10 and 11, respectively.
- *Financial Health* is about having adequate access to the financial resources necessary to thrive—resources that can provide a cushion during times of disruption and open paths to opportunity. It's also about attitudes and practices around money, and about having financial literacy.

- *Financial Health* isn't about a high-salary. Confusing *Financial Health* with just income is a mistake that many people make, and that mistake can actually lead to poor financial decisions, and ultimately very poor *Financial Health*.
- There is an epidemic of poor *Financial Health* in the U.S., and it's causing more and more people to become trapped in *decisions of desperation* rather than having access to *Courageous Leaps*.
- The five steps for cultivating *Financial Health* are:
  1. Let go of financial shame
  2. Face your truth about money, and the truth about money in your life
  3. Set specific goals and plans around your truth about money
  4. Cultivate your financial literacy
  5. Commit to a long-term practice of *Financial Health* check-ups

## Key Questions to Think About

1. How healthy is your relationship with money?
2. Do you have emergency savings to support you and your family during a disruption in income? How long would that savings last?
3. Do you have a financial plan that is built around your long-term goals?
4. How financially literate are you, and how are you cultivating further financial literacy?
5. How often do you perform "check-ups" on your *Financial Health*?

CHAPTER TEN

# BUILDING INTELLECTUAL CAPITAL

We've already examined the *Four Forces of Change* at work in this latest *fourth industrial revolution* (see Chapter 1) and how those forces are impacting jobs and careers for individuals. On a macro level, those forces (along with the scale and pace of change) are leading to a world that places a very high premium on an additional kind of wealth: *Intellectual Capital*.

Like *Financial Health*, *Intellectual Capital* unlocks access to opportunity. When faced with disruption and uncertainty, people who lack sufficient *Intellectual Capital* will find themselves with far fewer options and thus at risk of being forced into *decisions of desperation*, rather than having the option of making *Courageous Leaps*.

Recognizing the emergence of *Intellectual Capital*, understanding its implications, and understanding how to build *Intellectual Capital* is a key part of cultivating a **Thriving Mindset**.

FIGURE 18

THE THREE TYPES OF WEALTH

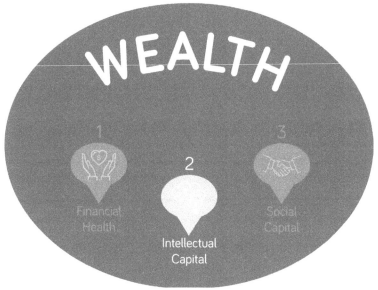

## THE SHIFT FROM A "KNOWLEDGE ECONOMY" TO A "LEARNING ECONOMY"

In 1966, the renowned business thinker and author Peter Drucker coined the terms "knowledge worker" vs. "manual worker" and described the difference between the two (Drucker, 2016). Manual workers create value through their direct manual labor, often in lines of work like manufacturing that produce a physical product. Knowledge workers create value by producing ideas and information. They include people like engineers, lawyers, physicians, business executives, information technologists, and other highly trained and high-skilled professionals. Drucker also popularized the idea of a "Knowledge Economy," referring to an economic system that places the highest value on the ideas and information produced by knowledge workers (Drucker, 2016). In Chapter 1, I discussed how the third industrial revolution—with the advent of digitization, mainframe computing, automation of manufacturing, and globalization—led to a knowledge economy in the United States. The emergence of that economy included significant gains for those in high-skilled professions and economic declines for manufacturing and middle America's manual workers.

The *Four Forces of Change*, and the speed at which they are proceeding, have now led to the next economic shift: the shift from a Knowledge Economy to a *Learning Economy*. Just as the transition to the knowledge economy meant economic upheaval—favoring knowledge workers and devaluing manual workers—the transition to a *Learning Economy* is bringing a similar transition. We are now in a world that places less value on sophisticated static skills (the skills that knowledge workers cultivate) and more value on the ability to learn quickly, acquire _new_ knowledge, and deploy that new knowledge in a dynamic environment. In short, a *Learning Economy* not only requires high levels of knowledge, but also the ability to update and expand that knowledge quickly.

Here are some components that illustrate the transition: By the year 2030, between 400 million and 800 million individuals could be displaced by automation (Jobs lost, jobs gained: What the future of work will mean for jobs, skills, and wages. Manyika, Lund, et al., 2017). Unlike the transition from manual worker to knowledge worker, this latest wave of change will impact all levels of the workforce, from the factory floor to the C-suite. McKinsey & Company has estimated that more than 20% of the activities consuming a CEO's work time could be automated with currently available technology (Chui, Manyika, and Miremadi, 2015). There are similar findings for a broad range of high-skilled, high-paid professions, like financial planners, physicians, attorneys, and many more. But these jobs won't be automated out of existence in the foreseeable future. Rather, advancements in technology will change the nature of these fields by offering sophisticated tools to increase productivity. In the near future, high-skilled knowledge workers will be expected to continually learn new technologies and skills in order to remain productive, competent, and competitive.

Advances in technology also create entirely new professions. Many of today's most in-demand jobs like "cloud specialist," "big-data architect," and "data scientist" didn't exist a decade ago. But these new jobs require new skill-sets. Also, new technologies—along with the opportunities they create—now come and go very quickly, so it's likely that people with advanced skills and knowledge will need to continually learn new skillsets throughout their careers. The solution is to focus on cultivating *Intellectual Capital*.

## THE FOUR COMPONENTS OF INTELLECTUAL CAPITAL

You can think of the *Intellectual Capital* that's needed to thrive in the emerging *Learning Economy* in four specific layers: **Foundational Knowledge, Critical Thinking, Social Intelligence,** and the ability to **Self-Educate.**

**Foundational Knowledge** includes basic competency in reading, language, math, and science, usually gained in early education. It also includes the specialized skills we gain in

**FIGURE 19**

**INTELLECTUAL CAPITAL**

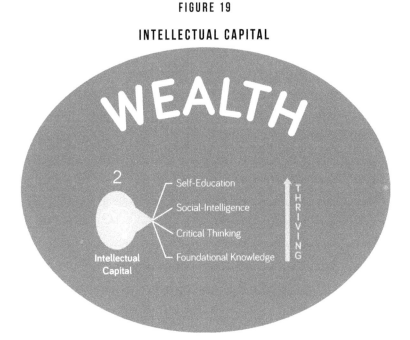

advanced and professional education, such as in college and postgraduate programs like law, business, medicine, technology, etc. Foundational knowledge supports all the other components of *Intellectual Capital* because it provides the base-line proficiency to be minimally productive in our avocations, and as citizens in society.

**Critical Thinking** is the ability to use foundational knowledge in new and unexpected situations. It's also the ability to operate with incomplete information and adapt to the unexpected. That's important in today's disruptive world because change comes quickly and is usually unpredictable. People will increasingly find themselves operating in very unfamiliar situations, so those with well-honed Critical Thinking skills are at an advantage.

**Social Intelligence** is the ability to connect and collaborate effectively with others. It's also the ability to form productive relationships with a diverse range of people, including people from different cultures. As we discussed in Chapter 1, the fourth force of change that's triggering disruption is a shrinking world. That means we are increasingly called upon to collaborate with people in different geographic locations and from different cultures. This makes social intelligence important because the people who are adept at functioning in complex, cross-cultural environments will be at a distinct advantage. Social intelligence also leverages "emotional intelligence" skills. (I'll explore more about social intelligence in the next chapter, "*Cultivating Social Capital.*")

**Self-Education** is the ability to continually increase your knowledge base. It's a recognition that static foundational knowledge is not sufficient in today's world. People with high self-education capabilities commit to an intentional process of constantly upgrading their knowledge and skill base, a practice of life-long learning.

## DEBATING THE VALUE OF HIGHER EDUCATION

Ironically, at the same time, as we evolve into a world that values the ability to learn—i.e., the cultivation of *Intellectual Capital*—there are parallel conversations in some quarters that question the value of higher education. Specifically, the value of investing in a college degree and beyond. Some of the debate is understandable. In the last 20 years, the cost of tuition has increased eight times faster than wages (Maldonado, 2018). In 2020, the average full cost of a four-year degree at a private non-profit institution (including tuition, fees, room, and board) was nearly $200,000 (Bustamante, 2019). Some institutions cost much more. For example, the total annual cost to attend Harvard University is currently more than $71,000 per year (National Center for Education Statistics, n.d.). The ever-rising costs have created a crisis of educational debt. As of 2020, outstanding student loan debt in the United States has reached $1.6 trillion and impacts 44.7 million Americans (Bastrikin, 2020). Student loan debt is now the second-highest consumer debt category, second only to mortgage debt, and surpassing credit card and auto loan debt.

Given these expenses and the considerable burden that excessive student loan debt places on college graduates (and the impact on their *Financial Health*), many people wonder if higher-education is worthwhile or even necessary. Some people highlight anecdotal stories about billionaires succeeding without a college degree, like Mark Zuckerberg. Some training programs promise market-ready technical job skills for a fraction of the cost of a college and in considerably less time than it would take to earn a four-year degree.

There is clearly a serious problem with the affordability and accessibility of higher education in the U.S. Everyone should have access to high-quality education without taking on crippling debt, and that issue needs to be addressed by both government and our higher education institutions. But, the debate about the *value* of education is different, and it's misguided. That's something I learned early on (because I experienced what I call *the transformative power of education*), and it's born out if you look at the long-term data.

## THE TRANSFORMATIVE, LIFE-CHANGING POWER OF EDUCATION

As I discussed earlier, I grew up as the son of a single mother. I knew my father, but he was an extremely contradictory presence in my life and sometimes a very damaging one. But he understood the power of *Intellectual Capital*, even if he wouldn't have called it by that term.

When I was born, my father Sydney was over 50 years old and already had a wife and two adult sons. He was an immigrant from an upper-middle-class Jamaican family and from a culture where it was common for men to have a "second family" outside of their marriage. That cultural practice was an extremely painful thing in my life because it was very clear that his "first family" was the priority, and ultimately his only real family. My mother always said that she didn't know about my father's wife and "first family" when they met.

My parents never lived together, but early on, my father would visit every couple of weeks to take me out. I longed for those visits because they were a respite from an otherwise chaotic home. My father clearly led a very different life than we did. His apartment was in a beautiful building, on a very nice block, with a doorman who always addressed my father as "Mr. Valentine." I walked by this building many times, but he rarely took me inside. (In retrospect, the times he took me inside were always when his wife was not at home.)

My father was always impeccably dressed, with a fedora, jacket, and tie, and he was always respectful in how he treated my mother. Literally the perfect image of a "gentleman"— even if he wasn't providing financial support. My father's world was a place where there seemed to be a sense of calm, security, and safety. There was never the fear that utilities were about to be shut off, and there was never a sense of disorder in his home. He was the first person to give me the idea that a very different life was possible—I just needed to "crack the code" on how to get there.

At the same time, my father was also extremely unreliable. At best, there was a 50/50 chance he'd show up when promised, and he frequently missed important occasions, like birthdays and holidays. When he didn't show, I was crushed. Sometimes I'd want to call and ask why, but my mother wouldn't allow it. She'd say I might "make trouble" for my father in his home. Young kids don't understand these dynamics, and for many years, I carried the idea that my existence could be the source of "trouble." My father never lived up to the responsibilities of parenting that many people take for granted—providing financial support, emotional support, or protection—and he was no longer interested in the demands of raising a child. By the time I was in high school, I understood the situation. I spent far less time with him, but I still idealized him. By the time I was in college, I rarely saw him, and I only saw him a handful of times after graduation. My college graduation was one of his infamous "no-shows." It was also the last time I'd ever invite him anywhere.

Despite his many shortcomings, there was one incredibly positive thing about him that has had a life-long impact on me: he understood the power of education and he instilled it in me. His family came from means, so he had an excellent education. His two sons from his marriage (my half-brothers) had been gifted academically—they had already graduated from college and were in successful careers. My father took pride in their accomplishments. Although he didn't spend much time with me, he noticed that I did very well in school. He saw and encouraged my talent in math and science. He too had an innate talent for math. My father was the first person to tell me that getting an education was the best path out of the neighborhood I lived in at that time. He explained that proving how smart I was would be the best way to combat the negative stereotypes and racism I would encounter as a Black man in the United States. Proving to him that I was smart and could do as well as my half-brothers became a way I tried to vie for his love and attention; it was also a way to show that I was just as worthy as his first-family.

My father was the one who found the private school that I ultimately attended on a scholarship. My mother didn't have the resources or connections to find an opportunity like that, although she was the one who paid the portion of the tuition that scholarships didn't cover—something that was an enormous stretch for her. When the time came for college, my father was also the one who encouraged me to think about "the Ivy Leagues," as he would put it. He said that an Ivy League-level of education would be the way to set myself apart. (It was also something that neither of my half-brothers had achieved.) Much to my father's credit, in high school, I always saw the smart kids as the "cool kids," so they became the crowd I wanted to hang out with the most. I was willing to do whatever it took to prove I belonged with that group and (by extension) that I also belonged in my father's world. That's how I ended up in the accelerated math program (taught by the maniacal soccer coach) and why I was so determined to succeed in class, whatever it took.

## HOW INTELLECTUAL CAPITAL OPENS DOORS OF OPPORTUNITY

The private school my father found was an enormous departure from the schools I'd previously attended. The educational opportunities it provided were light-years beyond what kids growing up in underprivileged neighborhoods, like mine, typically have access to, and an early taste of what it means to cultivate *Intellectual Capital.*

I would attend that school from 6<sup>th</sup> through 12<sup>th</sup> grade, and the experience literally changed the trajectory of my entire life. As I've discussed in other sections of this book, there were many difficult things about those early years. Being a low-income "scholarship kid"—and one who's from a troubled home—in an exclusive private school is a tough experience. It was not the kind of place where you're going to get much understanding, sympathy, or peer support. But the hard times there were well worth it.

Most of my classmates were from extremely privileged families, which meant the quality of the academics was extraordinary. With an extensive range of offerings—several languages, computer science, advanced math, literature, multiple types of history, arts, and music—we were expected to select classes that aligned with our interests. That system allowed me to take five years of math and six years of science in just four years of high school. It was fine to "double-up" as long as you could handle the work. I also learned two computer programming languages while still in high school—and this was the 1970s, long before most kids would have even touched a computer. Classes were small (typically no larger than 15 students), we were expected to actively participate, and teachers encouraged critical thinking. It wasn't about just getting the right answer—you were expected to explain your reasoning, debate ideas, and be creative.

The school's approach was enormously successful. Out of my class of 47 students (which was large by the school's standards), everyone went on to college. Roughly half went to what would be considered "elite schools" by today's standards, and almost a third went to Ivy League schools. The reason people did so well was because the entire system was based on the idea that learning should be its own reward. We weren't just being crammed with facts. We were being trained to think critically and creatively, to understand the value and power of knowledge, and to understand that we bore responsibility for our own education—in short, we were being taught to cultivate our *Intellectual Capital*. Colleges recognized that. Today, 35 years later, the alumni list includes a myriad of success stories—business leaders, attorneys, judges, authors, college professors, artists, entrepreneurs, and many others.

As important as the school was for my highly privileged peers, it was far more important for me. It opened doors of opportunity that I otherwise would never have known existed: after six years there, I was able to get into every college I applied to, and the benefits were much more than just that. The doors continued to open for decades to come, and they led to a life that I couldn't have fully imagined in those early years.

That's a key thing about *Intellectual Capital*: just as with other forms of wealth, *Intellectual Capital* opens doors. It allows you to take the *Courageous Leaps* that lead to opportunity, and it protects you from being forced into *decisions of desperation.* Kids who come from low-income neighborhoods (like the one I did) typically don't do well academically. They're faced with over-crowded classes, under-funded schools, and overwhelmed teachers. They also come to school burdened with a myriad of social issues that poverty breeds. They get little opportunity to cultivate the foundation of *Intellectual Capital* that will be so critical for opening doors of opportunity later in life, so cycles of poverty (another form of the *Adversity-Fear-Paralysis Cycle*) continue unabated through generations.

## ANSWERING THE DEBATE ABOUT EDUCATION IN A LEARNING ECONOMY

All of this, of course, brings me back to the current-day debate over the value of education. Here's why the debate is so misguided:

- If you think getting an education is expensive, try not having one. The average four-year college graduate (a person who earned a Bachelor's degree but who has no further degrees) will earn $1 million more in his or her working lifetime (defined as between age 24 and 64) than the average high school graduate (Carnevale, Rose, and Cheah, 2011).
- The incremental earnings increase dramatically as you cultivate more *Intellectual Capital.* The average person who goes on to earn a professional degree (such as an MBA, JD, or medical degree) will earn $2.3 million more in their working lifetime than the average high school graduate (Carnevale, Rose, and Cheah, 2011).

- The differential for cultivating more Intellectual Capital is increasing as we move into the *Learning Economy*. In 1980, the "wage premium" for having a college degree (defined as the difference between annual earnings for a college graduate vs a high school graduate) was $15,800 per year (Bahney, 2019). By 2018, the wage premium had more than doubled to $31,900 per year (Bahney, 2019).

- You can think of investing in *Intellectual Capital* as analogous to investing in financial wealth because (like financial wealth) the benefits of *Intellectual Capital* compound over time. Looking at the increase in average lifetime earnings, the rate-of-return on the average cost of a Bachelor's degree turns out to be 14% (Bahney, 2019). If you were to invest the same money in market securities, you could expect to see an average return of somewhere between 3% (for bonds) and 7% (for stocks) (Bahney, 2019). So, from a financial standpoint, investing in a four-year Bachelor's degree is literally one of the best investments you can make.

As for the anecdotal examples like Mark Zuckerberg, there will always be exceptions—but they are not the rule. And we should remember that Zuckerberg dropped out of Harvard, not high school. In fact, Harvard may have actually made it possible for him to launch Facebook to such success because the initial site was developed while he was at Harvard and as a tool for other students (Carlson, 2010). Zuckerberg also came from a background that afforded him the opportunity to get into Harvard in the first place—a home with well-educated parents who could afford to hire people to tutor their son on computer programming while

Zuckerberg was still in high school. Zuckerberg also attended college-level classes on computer science while still in high school. The average person who skips college is not likely to become the next Zuckerberg—they are far more likely to end up cleaning the floors in Zuckerberg's office and struggling financially.

Although higher education is a crucial piece of the puzzle, it's important to remember that the cultivation of *Intellectual Capital* requires more than just earning degrees. It's about continually cultivating your talents, building your ability to thrive in a highly-disruptive world, and ultimately building your ability to function as a productive world-citizen. People who fail to invest in building *Intellectual Capital*, and who fail to continually cultivate more *Intellectual Capital*, will find themselves left behind and unable to access opportunity.

## CULTIVATING INTELLECTUAL CAPITAL ISN'T ABOUT CHASING THE LATEST FAD

Here's one more thing to remember about cultivating *Intellectual Capital*: It's not just about following the latest fad or trying to take short cuts. That's analogous to trying to cultivate *Financial Health* by jumping on the latest "get-rich-quick" scheme. The obsession right now about equipping people with STEM (science, technology, engineering, and math) skills is an example of a short-cut that has concerned me.

Some have taken the obsession to an extreme. In 2011, Florida Governor Rick Scott announced his intention to direct state funds for education towards STEM programs, and away from the liberal arts and social sciences. Scott was quoted as saying, "We don't need a lot more anthropologists in the state... I want to spend our dollars giving people science, technology, engineering, math degrees... so when they get out of school, they can get a job." (Zaloom, 2019)

Although STEM skills are extremely valuable, they are not the end-all, be-all skill. I, myself, have a STEM degree, I worked in STEM-related fields for a significant part of my corporate career, and the degree proved to be an extremely beneficial asset. I thoroughly enjoyed getting my STEM degree because, at the time, I was very interested in the subject matter. I also have tremendous admiration for the STEM fields, and I'm very concerned about the lack of scientific literacy in the United States. However, _just_ equipping people with STEM skills—rather than engaging in full and ongoing cultivation of _Intellectual Capital_—is insufficient. Shuttling people into narrowly-conceived STEM training in this way deprives them of the ability to adapt and change through time, as new fields emerge and new skills are needed.

Let's think through Governor Scott's stance: although people with STEM degrees _initially_ out-earn their counterparts in liberal arts fields, the advantage fades steadily after the first job. By age 40, liberal arts majors have caught up (Deming, 2019). After that, graduates with liberal arts training go on to out-earn their pure-STEM counterparts. It's a dynamic I've experienced in my own career and one that I've seen in many technology-career clients that I've worked with in my coaching practice. Let's think through _why_.

When I graduated with my Bachelor's degree in Electrical and Computer Engineering, it was easy to find a job, and one that paid significantly more than jobs my liberal arts friends were landing. That was true even though I took a job outside of engineering—a management training job—simply because employers were so enamored with engineering degrees.

But the world shifted. When I thought about moving up the corporate ladder, it became clear that the engineering degree had diminished appeal. Some people even viewed it as a liability—thinking that it meant that my capabilities were limited to narrow technical thinking and that I'd struggle in broader, more strategic domains. That was a very big reason why I decided to pursue an MBA soon after college, and why I also decided on an MBA in marketing. I intentionally chose a discipline that would offset and complement (not duplicate) my prior highly technical training. That's one aspect of building *Intellectual Capital*: intentionally cultivating diverse skillsets over a life-time, because it's the diversity of skill (and thinking) that opens the doors of opportunity.

I've coached many mid-career technology professionals who find themselves in a bind. They pursued a narrow STEM discipline in their education—most of them long before it was even called "STEM." They've spent many years sticking doggedly to a technology track in their professional development. They might argue that they've cultivated *Intellectual Capital* because they've kept up with newer technologies in their field. But they now find themselves competing with younger professionals, most of whom are just as skilled on the newer technologies, if not more so. The skills these middle-aged, mid-career tech-folks learned over the years are outdated, and so that experience is irrelevant. The root problem is that many of them have stayed too narrow—both in their thinking and in their professional development. They haven't taken time to broaden their capabilities; to learn more about business and leadership; or to work on soft skills like communication, strategy, and critical thinking. They haven't branched out to explore other interests or talents—things that would put them in a more advantageous position. Had they done so, they would have been prepared for more senior levels in the organization or for a move into a different field.

It's always a challenge when I find clients in this situation because of another principle of *Intellectual Capital*: cultivating *Intellectual Capital* takes a long-term commitment—it's not something people can do overnight. These mid-career professionals often find themselves stuck in the kinds of *decisions of desperation* we discussed earlier—like staying in a job they dislike—at least for a time.

Here's the warning I give people who think narrowly-conceived STEM careers are the place to find safety in a disruptive world: I worry that we're creating the "factory welders" of tomorrow. A generation ago, becoming a factory welder was a ticket to a good-paying job and a comfortable middle-class life. It was a highly technical skill—people invested years in honing the expertise, and they expected lifetime employment. Then automation came along, with factory robots that can outperform human welders. Many STEM professionals are at risk of the same thing as computers get smarter and better. It's fine to start off with a STEM education, as I did—especially if you have a genuine interest in the field. But you have to realize that's not enough. You have to quickly and continually up-skill from there—you have to learn how to cultivate *Intellectual Capital*.

## THE SURPRISING SKILL GAPS IN THE LEARNING ECONOMY

Much of today's change and disruption are driven by technological advancement, and thus many people believe succeeding in the *Learning Economy* is purely about having technical skills. But that's an incomplete picture. Recent research into global employment trends, and the skill gaps that industry leaders are encountering, yields some interesting insight. Yes, technological skills are in high demand, but in many cases, they're just seen as foundational—the real skill gaps are in the area of soft skills (Burner, et al., 2019).

A study conducted in 2018 by McKinsey on employment trends in the United States and the EU shows us that the advent of "smarter" technology is causing an increase in demand for not only technical skills but also for social and emotional skills, as well as higher-cognitive skills (Bughin, et al., 2018). According to a 2019 study by the Society for Human Resources Management (SHRM), HR professionals are reporting difficulty recruiting job candidates with the necessary "soft-skills" for the job at hand (Burner, et al., 2019). Some of the leading soft-skill areas cited include creativity, problem-solving, critical thinking, the ability to deal with ambiguity, and communication. Also, as companies become more diverse, and as business becomes increasingly global, there is increased demand for people with the social and communication skills to build productive working relationships across different cultures, geographies, and borders.

## HOW TO PREPARE FOR THE LEARNING ECONOMY

Successfully preparing for the *Learning Economy* means reimagining our approach to education in general. Our current thinking on education prepares people for the world of the past, not the world of the future. That's because our definition of an education is out of step with today's realities.

In the past, an education was something you acquired in the first 18 to 25 years of life (depending on your avocation). It provided you with a very specific set of skills, and those skills were largely sufficient to make you productive and employable through your working lifetime, which would be the next 30 to 40 years.

That's no longer a realistic proposition. As we have learned, careers are being extended into much later in life, and the world is transforming around us at lightning speed, so people need to adapt to multiple waves of dramatic change during their working lifetimes.

Acquiring the knowledge to be productive, employable, and valuable can no longer be seen as a static, one-time process. In order to thrive in a *Learning Economy*, people need to embrace an ongoing, dynamic, and life-long process of continually gaining new knowledge and skills to meet the demands of an ever-changing world. Thriving in a *Learning Economy* requires the cultivation of *Intellectual Capital*.

## AN ADDITIONAL PERSONAL NOTE ABOUT INTELLECTUAL CAPITAL

There's an additional personal note I will make about cultivating *Intellectual Capital*: The act of writing this book—and in fact, becoming a writer at all—was an exercise in cultivating *Intellectual Capital* and especially *Self-Education*. Because I went to engineering school as an undergraduate, I had almost no training in writing. I haven't taken an English class since high school, and I could probably count the number of papers I wrote in college on my fingers, literally. Business school includes writing, but it's a very specific kind of writing and not the training I needed for writing a book. During my corporate career I tended to focus on more technical areas, and ones that required only minimal writing.

However, after I launched my business, it became obvious that writing was something that's important for people in my field. That included writing my own blogs, writing articles for publications, and ultimately writing this book. The process included investing in additional skill development, additional training, being uncomfortable sometimes, and even hiring a writing coach—all at a fairly late stage of my professional career. But that's the whole point: done correctly, the process of cultivating *Intellectual Capital* never ends. *The Thriving Mindset* requires a life-long commitment to learning.

I'll say more about that process (along with some of the additional challenges of writing this book) in Chapter 12 (The *Journey to Self-Acceptance*).

## CHAPTER SUMMARY—PUTTING IT ALL TOGETHER

In this chapter we discussed the second component of *Wealth*: *Intellectual Capital*. Like *Financial Health*, *Intellectual Capital* opens doors of opportunity, and enables people to take *Courageous Leaps*. And, just as we've discussed before, people who lack *Intellectual Capital* are at risk of being forced into *"decisions of desperation."*

### Some Key Points to Remember

- *Intellectual Capital* has become important because of the *Four Forces of Change* that are driving the *Fourth*

*Industrial Revolution.* These forces are leading to a new, *Learning Economy*, where the ability to quickly acquire new knowledge and adapt to change is in high demand.

- *Intellectual Capital* has four components:
  1. Foundational Knowledge—typically the skills we learn in formal education.
  2. Critical Thinking—the ability to use foundational knowledge in new and unfamiliar situations.
  3. Social Intelligence—the ability to connect and collaborate with highly diverse groups of people.
  4. Self-education—the ability to continually amass new skills and add to foundational knowledge.

- We need to re-think our traditional view of what it means to gain an education. Education is no longer just something you acquire in early life. The pace of change causes old skills to become obsolete more quickly than ever before. We now need to think of education as a dynamic, life-long process of continually cultivating *Intellectual Capital*.

- Ironically, at the same time that the ability to learn is becoming more valuable, there's a parallel debate about the value of higher education, given the very high cost. High-cost withstanding, life-time earnings data shows that higher education is, on average, one of the best financial investments available. The payback is likely to increase as we move further into a *Learning Economy*, and technology subsumes even more traditional "working class" occupations.

## Key Questions to Think About

1. How much emphasis are you currently placing on increasing your *Intellectual Capital*?

2. How proficient are you in the four components that make up *Intellectual Capital*—Foundational Knowledge, Critical Thinking, Social Intelligence, and Self-Education Skills?

3. How comfortable are you that your current skill sets will remain in demand amid the disruption of further technological advancement?

4. What are three things you could do to commit to lifelong learning and further cultivate your own *Intellectual Capital*?

CHAPTER ELEVEN

# CULTIVATING SOCIAL CAPITAL

On October 12, 2019, a Kenyan runner by the name of Eliud Kipchoge accomplished something spectacular: He became the first man to run the 26.2-mile marathon distance in less than two hours (Keh, 2019). His time—of 1 hour, 59 minutes, and 40 seconds—smashed the symbolic "2-hour barrier" that many people believed would never be broken. Even for a runner as talented as Kipchoge—who had previously set the marathon world record of 2 hours, 1 minute, and 39 seconds—it was a remarkable feat.

Kipchoge's sub-2-hour time doesn't qualify as a new "world record" because records need to be set in competitions, and this wasn't actually a race. It was a solo event, set up as four laps on a six-mile course on the streets of Vienna, and sponsored by Nike, Inc. The goal was to test whether a human was capable of running that fast over the marathon distance.

But even though this wasn't a race, Kipchoge didn't run alone. He was assisted by a total of 42 other runners who were organized in groups of seven, each of which took turns running along with Kipchoge (Detrixhe, 2019). Five would run in front of him, and two would run alongside him. Together they formed a "V" around Kipchoge to decrease aerodynamic resistance, set a reliable pace, and offer encouragement. And of course, to keep up the 4:32 minute per mile pace required, the other runners in Kipchoge's platoon were themselves some of the world's best athletes. There were several Olympic medal holders, hailing from far-flung countries, including Kenya, Japan, Uganda, Ethiopia, and Norway.

Distance running is a notoriously solitary sport, with marathon runners in particular logging immense numbers of solo miles. But Kipchoge didn't see it that way when he looked back on this event. Kipchoge said that the other men who'd run in front of him and beside him were "among the best runners of all time" and that their efforts were what had made the amazingly fast run time possible. Kipchoge's accomplishment—and in fact, the entire way this event was organized—is an excellent metaphor for the third kind of wealth that's critical for *The Thriving Mindset*: *Social Capital*.

When I talk about *Social Capital*, people sometimes think about "social climbing" or stereotypical "networking." That's not what cultivating *Social Capital* is about. That view is completely off the mark. In fact, in many ways, that's the exact opposite of *Social Capital*. *Social Capital* is about surrounding yourself with people who inspire you, who bring out the best in you, and who encourage you to achieve more than you would have thought possible on your own. People whom you, in turn, inspire and encourage. It's about

## FIGURE 20

## THE THREE TYPES OF WEALTH

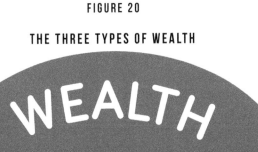

cultivating mutually beneficial, authentic, and uplifting relationships. Sometimes these relationships will be friendships, but they aren't only limited to friendships.

## SOCIAL CAPITAL IN THE BUSINESS WORLD

Several years ago, I had a client who understood *Social Capital* very well. His name is Ben, and he was the founder and CEO of a very successful tech start-up. Ben believed that a major part of any entrepreneur's job is to build out their (metaphorical) "Rolodex" because, as an entrepreneur, sooner or later, you will encounter a problem you don't know how to solve. In those moments, your success (or failure) depends on whether you know someone who can help.

Ben was right, but the concept isn't limited to entrepreneurs. No matter what your avocation—whether
self-employed, an executive in a large company, a non-profit
leader, or anything else—at some point, you're going to
encounter a problem you don't know how to solve, and your
ability to leverage your *Social Capital* will determine your
success or failure.

## SOCIAL CAPITAL HAS A BIG IMPACT ON YOUR COMPETENCE

Some people are uncomfortable with the idea of cultivating *Social Capital* because they believe it sounds like "playing politics" rather than being competent and letting your
accomplishments speak for themselves—i.e., the old "it's not
what you know, it's who you know" saying. That is not correct. *Cultivating Social Capital* is ultimately about increasing
your competence.

The thing that will determine how well you thrive amid
disruption is definitely what you know. In fact, what you
know is especially important for the kind of disruption in
the emerging fourth industrial revolution, with the increased
value of knowledge and *Intellectual Capital.*

However, _who_ you know has a very large impact on
_what_ you know. That's because we gain a great deal of our
competence from the people with whom we interact. When
we cultivate *Social Capital* correctly, our contacts provide
us with new insight, and they inspire us to grow intellectu-
ally. That expanded knowledge will, in turn, determine how
successful we are in our endeavors, and in many cases, our
connections will determine whether or not we gain access

to important opportunities. People who become isolated lose access to vital information and intellectual growth, and their competency ultimately degrades. In the end, your success is indeed determined by what you know and your competency. But who you know has a very significant impact on what you know.

The people who are the most successful—the ones who get the best assignments, have the best results, and seemed to get promotion after promotion—are rarely socially isolated. They typically have extensive networks, well-placed mentors, and advocates in important places. They leverage their connections to get advice, steer through difficult situations, become aware of emerging opportunities and risks, and even to exert influence. They provide the people in their networks with the same type of help and support in return.

In short, the people who are the most successful are generally the ones who have the most other people helping them. The people who neglect to cultivate their *Social Capital* are left laboring in isolation and obscurity.

## SOCIAL CAPITAL IN A HIGHLY INTERCONNECTED WORLD

There's another reason why cultivating *Social Capital* is essential for the new world that's emerging. The highly interconnected and shrinking world that's being ushered in by the Internet and social media means that we operate in larger and more complex communities than ever before. In the past, a social misstep had limited impact. Today, a poorly chosen statement, text, or video can potentially rocket around the world at the speed of light. We've all been witness to people who've damaged their reputations and careers because of something that a decade ago would have been quickly forgotten.

Because the Internet collapses geographic barriers, we now also interact in far more diverse communities than ever before. The act of cultivating *Social Capital* also sharpens the social skills that lead to more effective interaction within this highly interconnected world. People who build the most effective *Social Capital* also take care to build-in the kind of diversity within their connections that aids in the effective cross-cultural collaboration that is increasingly prevalent in today's world. In fact, the diversity aspect of cultivating *Social Capital* was also reflected in Kipchoge's marathon accomplishment. You'll recall that I mentioned the runners alongside him came from far-flung countries like Kenya, Japan, Uganda, Ethiopia, and Norway. That's because the ability to run at this speed is a very rare talent. In order to assemble 40 people capable of running that fast, you need to recruit from around the world. Just as with Kipchoge, we too need to cultivate broad and diverse social networks in order to maximize the talent pool we can access.

## THE THREE TYPES OF CONNECTIONS YOU NEED TO BUILD SOCIAL CAPITAL

There are three specific kinds of relationships to keep in mind when cultivating *Social Capital*: *Social Relationships*, *Tactical Relationships*, and *Growth Relationships*.

**Social Relationships** are the easiest to understand. They are our friends, the people we enjoy spending time with. Virtually everyone creates social connections.

**FIGURE 21**

**SOCIAL CAPITAL**

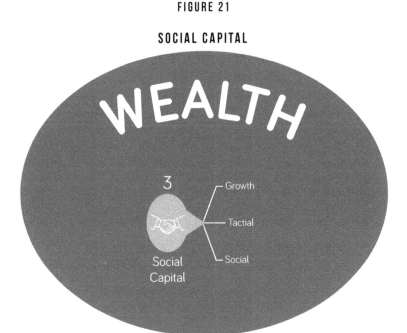

**Tactical Relationships** are the people we need to know in order to function in our day-to-day lives. They are our co-workers, our bosses, business partners, service providers, and anyone else we need to know to get our daily work done. Most people also have a well-established network of tactical connections.

**Growth Relationships** are the area that many people neglect. They are people who are outside of our day-to-day life process, and they may not necessarily be friends. They are the people who can give us access to new insights and new ways of thinking. They might be the people you meet on a special project or while volunteering for a charity. The people I met while in business school are an excellent example of growth network opportunities, and that's the kind of opportunity that too many people allow to fall by the wayside.

Social, tactical, and growth relationships are often dynamic and overlapping, so that sometimes individuals can represent more than just one kind of connection. Someone you meet during a special project, and who becomes a great growth connection, can also grow into a close friend. Likewise, you may discover that some friendships also become growth relationships over time.

## SOCIAL CAPITAL AND INTROVERTS

Whenever I discuss cultivating *Social Capital*, I always make a point to mention "introverts." The thought of cultivating *Social Capital* can be daunting for people who consider themselves to be introverts, but there's no reason why that needs to be the case. Although the exact number is hard to verify, introverts are thought to make up 25 to 40% of the population (Cherry, 2019), so that's a lot of people who could potentially count themselves out of this important asset. In fact, I, too, am an introvert. We introverts can be just as effective as our extrovert peers at building *Social Capital*. It's just a matter of honoring our introvert tendencies and taking care to cultivate our *Social Capital* in ways that are aligned with our strengths and needs.

The important thing is to understand what it means to be introverted and dispel some myths. Most importantly, being introverted doesn't mean that you don't like people or that you're necessarily shy or socially awkward. Introverts can be as social as anyone else; it's just that socializing tends to be draining for introverts. Our extroverted counterparts, on the other hand, tend to find social interaction energizing, and they can find it draining to be left on their own.

For introverts to build *Social Capital*, we simply need to find situations and spaces that work well for our tendencies and our strengths. For example, like many introverts, I'm not a fan of big cocktail parties and happy hours. I find them completely overwhelming and exhausting. That's because I like to focus very intently on one person at a time, to give them my full attention, and really listen to what they are saying. That tendency works out really well in one-on-one situations. Like many introverts, I'm great at listening and forming strong, close relationships. It's a strength that my executive coaching clients really appreciate. When it comes to cultivating *Social Capital* and building the relationships I need, I focus more on getting to know people deeply in smaller settings, rather than mass gatherings. Anyone who looks at my calendar will quickly recognize that I spend a lot of time in "coffee get-togethers." That's fine with me because that's how I enjoy getting to know people.

If you're an introvert, you'll need to place intentional focus on cultivating *Social Capital*. But don't try to do it the way that your extroverted friends might. Find ways to establish and build relationships that work for you and that leverage your strengths.

## FIND PEOPLE WHO WILL LIFT YOU UP

When I was in college, I joined a fraternity. It's something I don't talk about often because of the horrible reputation fraternities can have, especially regarding the treatment of women. (To the best of my knowledge, there was never an incident of harassment or abuse of women in my fraternity.) There were a lot of ways in which my fraternity was different from the stereotypical "frat house." We definitely weren't a "jock-house." In fact, I don't remember any college athletes in the house. However, there were a disproportionately high number of engineers and pre-meds—that alone probably speaks volumes about the house.

We had an "initiation weekend" every year, although, nothing that would qualify as some of the "hazing" stories that have become all too common. A lot of what went on could (almost) qualify as an extreme form of corporate "team-building." However, there was also a fair amount of alcohol available for those who chose to drink. The drinking age was 18 back then, but there were also a number of house members who didn't drink—again, not the stereotypical frat. The real goal of fraternity initiation (if it's done right) is to build a sense of camaraderie between the members of the incoming class.

One of the activities during initiation weekend was called "the wall." Our house had a two-story stone wall in the back that led up from the yard to a porch. There were twelve members in my "pledge class," and the assignment was that we needed to scale the wall—as a group. If anyone was left behind, then the entire group "failed." This was also a couple of years before I would lose my excess weight. I was still close to 250 lbs. and not at all athletic. I was stunned and instantly knew there was absolutely no way I could do it. I wondered if I could drop out of initiation right then so that I wouldn't take the rest of my pledge class (who were my friends by then) down with me. But the other eleven in my class wouldn't hear of it. They insisted that (with everyone's help) I could scale this wall. We developed a plan for me to go near the beginning of the group. That way, there were enough people still below to lift me up, and a few up to help me over. Then others could hang on to me at the top while I pulled some of the mid-sized guys up. I will never forget the feeling of being lifted up that wall by eleven other people that I trusted.

Before my college days, I'd never experienced anything remotely like that. As I discussed in earlier chapters, in high school, my "friends" were the "smart kids" because I believed it was cool to be smart. But they weren't actually friends by any healthy meaning of the word. Typically, they were highly privileged kids, and they were keenly aware that I didn't fit into their world—something they took every occasion to let me know. A better word for the relations was "peer group;" one that was never fully accepting and sometimes even hostile. I was fortunate that my high school has a zero-tolerance policy for violence (literally fights didn't happen), so there wasn't any physical bullying. But the put-downs and ridicule were nearly constant.

By the time I was in 9th grade, I was also starting to realize that I was gay, although I didn't fully understand what that meant. I just knew that I was extremely attracted to other boys. I even developed a couple of heart-breaking crushes on some of the boys at school. I also knew that this was something I had to keep secret at all cost. This was well before there would have been any support for "coming out" in high school. Back then, there were no notable gay role models. It had only been eight years since the Stonewall Uprising in 1969 (an event that's considered to be a major turning point in the modern LGBTQ rights movement) and LGBTQ people were regularly assaulted or killed for being open about their identities. I also knew that both my mother and father were extremely homophobic, so I couldn't expect any acceptance or support from them. It was a time when I was utterly alone, on many fronts.

That takes me back to the fraternity part of the story. Things got much better at Cornell, and it was because of *Social Capital*. I largely put being gay out of my mind for the first two years of college—that was not always easy when living with 45 other men, but the demands of college life helped. I dated a couple of women very casually, to keep up appearances, but managed to minimize the physical part of those relationships. By the middle of my junior year, I was once again head-over-heels-in-love with a friend—but this time, he was a "real" friend. I knew by this time that I could either "deal" with being gay—whatever that meant—or my life was going to spiral out of control. I was also sure that the stress of this secret was going to cause me to fail out of school and very likely lose my mind.

But a great deal had changed by that point—most notably, I was no longer alone. Getting up that wall during the initiation weekend was just the first of many times we needed to lift each other up. We'd lived together, managed a house together, dined together, stressed-out together about finals and finances, and navigated the path towards adulthood. There had been some really tough times, some amazingly joyful times, and admittedly, some times of not exercising the best judgment. Most importantly, I had intentionally chosen this group, and they had intentionally chosen me. It was the first time in my life I felt like I belonged, and that I was valued.

Being in the fraternity gave me the *Social Capital* I needed to succeed academically—away from home for the first time, and in a very demanding environment—and it also gave me something more. Ironically, being in this stereotypically straight-male setting of a fraternity is what gave me the self-confidence to come out. It was still difficult and frightening, but my experience in the house had taught me that I could be accepted and valued. Even if the worst happened, and my fraternity brothers rejected me because I was gay, I now had the self-confidence to know that I could find another place where I'd be accepted and valued.

The worst didn't happen! In fact, it was a wonderful experience. To be fair, I didn't tell everyone in the house, and there were some (about five of them) who definitely wouldn't have taken the news well. But I'd chosen my closest friends very carefully. They were surprised, but no one reacted negatively, and they kept the news confidential. I even told the friend of mine who I'd had the crush on. He is straight, so he couldn't return my feelings, but we stayed friends. (I still have a picture of us from my senior year, standing arm in arm, and he fully aware that I'm gay. It's a wonderful memory.)

Here's the lesson I learned from my fraternity years, and it's one that's critical for cultivating *The Thriving Mindset*: If you want to thrive through the difficult, disruptive times, you need to surround yourself with the people who will "lift you up." They are:

1. The people who see you for who you are, value you for who you are and value you for the things you like about yourself.
2. The people who will encourage you to excel, overcome, and grow. Sometimes that will be in ways that surprise both you and them. Certainly, my coming out was growth in a way that surprised my fraternity friends, but they encouraged me all the same.
3. The people who you respect, value, and want to lift up.

There's another aspect of these special relationships that people sometimes get wrong: the people who lift us up (and whom we, in turn, lift up) are not necessarily just like us. In fact, sometimes they are very different from us, but the difference is expressed in a way that enriches you both. I was very different from many of my fraternity friends. Today, some of my closest friends are very different from me—and our differences enrich our friendship.

My high school peer group served a tactical purpose— they gave me a way to understand (and ultimately access) a world of opportunity that was very different than the one I had been born into. But those weren't positive or uplifting relationships—in fact they led to some very isolated, lonely, and hurtful times—but I survived and moved on. Sometimes we need to endure (and survive) sub-optimal relationships in our lives because those relationship serve a tactical purpose. That's okay, as long as these relationships are finite. However, the focus should be on populating our lives with the people who lift us up; that's the *Social Capital* that's necessary to move into *The Thriving Mindset*.

## CHAPTER SUMMARY—PUTTING IT ALL TOGETHER

In this chapter, we discussed the final component of *Wealth*: *Social Capital*. Like *Financial Health* and *Intellectual Capital*, *Social Capital* opens doors to the opportunities that enable *Courageous Leaps*. People who lack *Social Capital* can also find themselves stuck because the connections we cultivate are an important source of knowledge and opportunity. That's why learning to cultivate *Social Capital* is an essential part of building a *Thriving Mindset*.

**Some Key Points to Remember:**

- *Social Capital* is not about "social climbing" or stereotypical "networking." In fact, that's the exact opposite of *Social Capital*. *Social Capital* is about surrounding yourself with people who inspire you, bring out the best in you, and encourage you to achieve.
- *Social Capital* is also always a two-way street; it's about developing authentic, two-way relationships with people whom you also support, inspire, and encourage in return.
- *Social Capital* is especially important in the business world because we get much of our competence from the people we know. When we encounter difficult or unfamiliar situations, we depend on our networks for advice and counsel.
- The people who are the most successful are rarely socially isolated. They typically have extensive networks, well-placed mentors, and advocates in important places.
- The highly interconnected world that's being ushered in by the Internet and social media means that we operate in larger and more complex communities than ever before. That places an even higher premium on the ability to cultivate *Social Capital*.
- *Social Capital* is composed of three different types of relationships that we need to cultivate:
  1. **Social Relationships:** Our friends and other people we enjoy spending time with.
  2. **Tactical Relationships:** The people we need to know in order to function in our day-to-day lives, like co-workers, our bosses, and anyone else we need to know to get our daily work done.

3. **Growth Relationships:** People outside of our day-to-day who can give us access to new insights and new ways of thinking.

- These three kinds of relationships that make up *Social Capital* are dynamic and evolving. For example, a relationship that starts as a Growth Relationship may evolve into a friendship (Social Relationship) over time.

- Some people believe that being an "introvert" precludes cultivating *Social Capital*, but that's not true. Introverts can be very good at building deeply authentic relationships, and *Social Capital* is about creating those deep, authentic relationships. Introverts need to focus on building relationships in a manner that is consistent with their nature, rather than trying to emulate "extroverts."

### Key Questions to Think About:

1. How much attention are you paying to cultivating your own *Social Capital*?
2. Are you cultivating authentic, two-way relationships where you are also supporting people in your network?
3. How many Growth Relationships do you have in your life, and how might you cultivate more?
4. If you're an introvert by nature, how might you leverage your inherent strengths to cultivate more *Social Capital*?

CHAPTER TWELVE

# THE JOURNEY TO
# SELF-ACCEPTANCE

The ability to accept ourselves, and value ourselves for who we are, is the one final tool for coping with change, disruption, and uncertainty. *The Journey to Self-Acceptance* is especially important at these times because when we don't accept ourselves (and fully value ourselves), that lack of acceptance becomes a kind of head wind or drag, and it can prevent us from taking *Courageous Leaps* into our full potential. *Self-Acceptance* may sound like a simple task, but it's not. Many people struggle to accept and value themselves, and the lack of *Self-Acceptance* is often a direct path into the *Adversity-Fear-Paralysis Cycle*.

Self-Acceptance can be especially challenging for people like me, who come from an underprivileged or marginalized group; that can include women, members of the LGBTQ community, racial minorities, people with disabilities, and anyone who is outside of the mainstream. That's because those of us outside of the majority can frequently encounter a chorus of negative messages that suggest we are somehow "less than." However, in my executive coaching practice, I've also learned that even people who are very much inside of the mainstream—people who may come from very privileged backgrounds and who may have an outside appearance of confidence—can also struggle with self-acceptance. In fact, most of the people I've worked with have struggled with self-acceptance at some point.

I believe the way to develop self-acceptance is to think of it as a journey that may unfold in stages. It's a journey that offers important lessons, opens the door to opportunities and, (most importantly) presents the *Courageous Leaps* that enable a *Thriving Mindset*.

## WHY I THOUGHT I COULD NEVER HAVE WRITTEN THIS BOOK

The biggest lesson I've learned about self-acceptance involved something that I've struggled with for most of my life. It's something I kept secret for many years and something that I once believed would prevent me from ever writing a book. That is the fact that I have a condition called dyslexia.

Most people think of dyslexia as the tendency to reverse words or letters—which does sometimes happen—however the symptoms can be far more complex, and the condition can manifest itself differently in different people. For some, the symptoms include slow reading speed and difficulty with spelling. Others may struggle to read at all; have difficulty organizing their thoughts when writing or speaking; and even have problems with spatial relationships, like when reading maps or understanding directions. Experts believe that

15 to 20% of the population have some degree of dyslexia (The International Dyslexia Association, n.d.), and there's no cure for the condition.

In my case, the symptoms of dyslexia are relatively mild. They are largely limited to slow reading, serious problems with spelling, and a near inability to proofread for typos. For many years I believed having dyslexia meant that certain pursuits were beyond my capabilities—pursuits like writing a book.

## MY SHAME ABOUT DYSLEXIA

There is a great deal of stigma attached to having dyslexia because it impacts fundamental literacy skills—the ability to read well and spell correctly—and many people *incorrectly* equate having dyslexia with ignorance and "illiteracy." It's common for people with dyslexia to harbor shame about the condition. Experts recommend that children at risk for dyslexia be tested as early as possible, usually around age five or six. A primary reason for that is to start supportive learning early and prevent the child from internalizing stigma about the condition. My dyslexia was diagnosed late, in the 10th grade, and I'd been struggling for many years. In fact, the reason I was tested was because a couple of teachers were baffled by the differences in my abilities. I was excellent at math and science—it was obvious I worked very hard and was committed to my studies—but I had serious problems with spelling and proofreading.

For most of my life, dyslexia has been a source of tremendous anxiety, insecurity, and shame. For example, during my corporate career, producing work with spelling errors would have had a serious impact on how I was perceived. In some circumstances, it could've cost me my job. Dyslexia was especially challenging in my early career, before word processors with spell-check had become ubiquitous, and before I had an administrative assistant to do my typing and proofreading. There were times when handing in an important work product was terrifying because I simply had no way of ensuring that everything was spelled correctly.

Here's one of the best examples, and it's something I struggle with to this day: I tend to misspell the same word in multiple places in the same paragraph, but each misspelling of the word is a different spelling. Sometimes the error is substituting a different word, but a wrong word that has a similar spelling, and thus something that spell-check won't catch. For example, substituting the word "form" for the word "from" is one of my most frequent mistakes.

When this happens, I have no idea there is an error, and I typically can't find the mistake, even after being told it's there. When someone who doesn't have or understand dyslexia (like a co-worker or boss) sees a mistake like this they're quick to assume you're lazy, sloppy, or illiterate. I also struggle with very slow reading, but most of my teachers never noticed that problem, because I hid it by putting in enormous amounts of time to get through reading assignments.

For people who can easily proofread this might sound minor, but there are few things more embarrassing than having your boss find a big spelling error on the first page of an important document. Even later in my career, when I'd achieved some level of seniority, I was still deeply embarrassed if someone who reported to me found typos or spelling mistakes in my work.

By the time I was diagnosed, I'd engrained the idea that my inability to spell and slow reading meant something was "wrong" with me. I kept that idea well into adulthood, and my dyslexia was something I went to great lengths to hide.

In addition to the emotional cost of carrying that degree of shame, there was also a practical cost. There are accommodations available for kids with learning differences like dyslexia when taking college entrance exams, and there are supportive services even through college. For example, students with dyslexia are often allowed extra time when taking exams. I didn't pursue any accommodations because I was too ashamed of needing them. My mother also didn't understand how to advocate on my behalf. Again, that's something that often results from being from a low-income family, with a parent who was already at her limit just trying to hold the home together.

My scores on college entrance exams showed the problem. I had excellent scores on math and science exams because I knew the subject matter, and those exams don't require much reading. However, my scores on exams that emphasized reading or verbal ability were much lower because I typically couldn't read the exams fast enough to make it through the tests.

I never revealed my dyslexia in college or graduate school and never took advantage of the accommodations that would have allowed me to better demonstrate my true abilities.

## COPING STRATEGIES AND SELF-IMPOSED LIMITATIONS

I also had my own "secret" coping strategies that I employed for the better part of four decades. In school, I avoided coursework that I perceived as reading- or writing-intensive and focused on the math and science that (for me) were much easier. That strategy allowed me to take more math and science in high school. It also gave me an excuse for avoiding some of the English and language classes because I'd already filled my schedule with courses that were perceived as very demanding. In four years of high school, I'd completed five years of math and six years of science, so no one questioned why I wasn't taking more language or history. In college, that same strategy led me to major in engineering and computer science—again, disciplines that most people consider extremely demanding, but that were easier for me. An engineering degree also turned out to be extremely marketable and lucrative. Business school tends to have a lot of group projects, so I became known as the person with excellent math, computer, and analytical abilities. That meant many of the people from non-quantitative backgrounds wanted to work with me on projects. They were happy to take on more of the writing if I took on the majority of the math, computer work, and analytics. In my early business career, I leaned towards jobs and assignments that required more computer and analytical ability and less writing.

The coping strategies largely worked. They hid most of the dyslexia, they allowed me to do very well in school and get very impressive degrees, and they allowed me to survive in a corporate career. But the strategies also came with a significant cost, both emotionally and practically. On the emotional side, I spent decades feeling like I was covering for what I couldn't do, rather than embracing and celebrating the extremely valuable talents I brought to the table. On the practical side, I avoided areas that would have been beneficial in the long-run, such as studying subjects like literature, philosophy, and history that would have provided me with a more well-rounded education and better development of the *Intellectual Capital* we discussed in Chapter 10.

Because my coping strategies were rooted in denying and hiding dyslexia, rather than accepting and embracing my learning difference, they caused me to impose limits on myself and my potential, and they ultimately cost me opportunity. Yes, I did very well for myself (especially under the circumstances), but the cost (both emotionally and practically) was much higher than it needed to be.

That's the problem with a lack of self-acceptance: It ultimately leads to self-imposed limitations. It's a problem I've seen many times in my executive coaching practice. People who do not accept something fundamental about themselves wind up imposing limits on their own potential. Those limits prevent them from taking *Courageous Leaps* into opportunity, which is especially important in times of change and disruption.

## THE BEGINNING OF SELF-ACCEPTANCE: CHALLENGING A SELF-IMPOSED LIMITATION

The *Journey to Self-Acceptance* around dyslexia began when I was forced to challenge one of my self-imposed limitations: my belief that I didn't like to write. I always assumed that people with dyslexia couldn't be good writers and that I would hate writing. I haven't taken an English class since high school, partially because the rigors of engineering school don't allow time for much other than the core curriculum, but also because of shame and the fear of being found out.

In graduate school and throughout my corporate career, I minimized the amount of writing I did and focused on my quantitative and analytical strengths, an approach that, in hindsight, I now realize also brought career limitations.

That had to change when I launched my executive coaching practice. Soon after starting my business, I learned that people in my industry often write blogs and other articles to showcase their expertise. I was determined for my business to succeed, so I gritted my teeth and committed to doing whatever was necessary to produce the required writing. That included hiring a writing coach. I also discovered that there are very inexpensive online proofreading services. The enormous shame I'd carried for decades about my inability to spell and proofread could be addressed for (literally) pennies a word, in just an hour or two, and with zero judgment.

The more important lesson was that I don't hate writing. In fact, I love writing, and I'm reasonably good at it, especially for someone with virtually no training as a writer.

One of my favorite writing experiences happened several years ago, when a friend suggested I submit an op-ed to a local paper, the *Boulder Daily Camera*. My husband and I were living in Boulder, Colorado, at the time, and I'd become known for having a unique perspective on many local issues. When I was introduced to the editorial page editor, I was transparent about my dyslexia. The editor said he didn't care about fixing typos. His exact quote was, "I fix typos all day." Instead, he was interested in the quality of my ideas and the clarity of my arguments. After reviewing a sample piece I'd drafted, he said, "If this is how you write, I'd rather have you do a regular column." I was shocked, flattered, and elated!

Writing for the *Boulder Daily Camera* was an enormous step. I continued with the paper for two years, until I moved back to New York City. The experience built my confidence, opened the door for me to write articles for several more publications, and ultimately paved the way for this book.

I learned a critical lesson by challenging my self-imposed limitation—my belief that dyslexia is an insurmountable impediment to writing. Good writing isn't about perfect spelling, punctuation, or grammar; none of which I have. Good writing is fundamentally about your ideas, and articulating those ideas effectively. I have lots of ideas. I love figuring out how to articulate those ideas with clarity, and I'm dedicated to putting in the work it takes. That makes me something I never knew I could be—a good writer. I would never have learned that without challenging the self-imposed limitation.

## THE STRENGTHS IN OUR WEAKNESSES: LEARNING TO ACCEPT (AND VALUE) DYSLEXIA

Sometimes the things we believe are our greatest limitations are, in reality, important strengths. That has turned out to be the case with dyslexia. Now, I accept and *value* it. I now realize this condition I once saw as a source of shame has, in reality, provided me with a unique set of important strengths. Discovering hidden strengths is the ultimate goal of self-acceptance.

My dyslexia was diagnosed almost four decades ago. But it took a very long time (well into adulthood) before I learned some important things about the condition. Part of the delay in learning about dyslexia was because of the shame and stigma associated with it. But the delay was also because we've only recently begun to better understand what dyslexia is and, more importantly, what it is not. Dyslexia is not a problem with vision; it's a difference in how the brain processes visual information. That word "difference" is important, and you may have noted that I've referred to dyslexia in this chapter as a learning "difference," _not_ as a learning disability.

Dyslexia is also not a deficiency in cognitive abilities or intelligence. On average, people with dyslexia have normal intelligence. However, a study conducted by the Cass School of Business in London has shown that people with dyslexia may also show increased abilities in certain areas (Bowers, 2007). Those areas can include complex problem solving and strategic thinking, mechanical reasoning, improved oral communication skills, better leadership and delegation skills, and increased creativity. As a result, people with dyslexia tend to be over-represented in fields like engineering, architecture, and the sciences; among creative people and artists; and among successful entrepreneurs and inventors. One of the most vocal advocates for people with dyslexia is Sir Richard Branson, a self-made multi-billionaire and founder of Virgin Atlantic Airways. Branson has dyslexia, and he believes that his dyslexia is what provided him with the creativity that made him a successful entrepreneur. Other well-known and highly successful people with dyslexia include Charles Schwab, founder of the discount brokerage that bears his name; John Chambers, chief executive of Cisco; Craig McCaw, the cellular phone pioneer; and Paul Orfalea, founder of the Kinko's copy chain (Griswold and Love, 2013).

For me, learning about the strengths dyslexia can offer was both insightful and familiar. I've always been extremely good at problem-solving and strategic thinking. This was a significant benefit during my corporate career and is now a tremendous benefit that I bring to my executive coaching clients. Likewise, mechanical reasoning is why I was so comfortable with math, science, and engineering. The oral communication abilities were there too. I've always been a good and comfortable public speaker. Perhaps more than anything else, I believe my dyslexia has given me the tenacity to find novel solutions when I face a tough problem. That kind of tenacity is something many dyslexic people seem to have and is something else that makes us good entrepreneurs; we've usually had to find novel ways around the hurdles that dyslexia presents.

Over the last several years, and as a result of learning more about the condition, my dyslexia evolved from something I went to great pains to hide to something that I now value. Of course, there are still struggles associated with the condition, but I'm also keenly aware of the benefits and abilities dyslexia has brought into my life. Like Sir Richard Branson, I've realized that I, too, likely owe much of my success to dyslexia.

Now, when I meet new clients or other business associates, I will often tell them upfront that I have dyslexia. This way, if they receive an email from me with a typo, they'll understand that it's not a sign of being sloppy or careless. I've also given keynote speeches (sometimes in front of hundreds of people) where I've spoken about having dyslexia and what it has brought to my life—both the negatives *and* the positives.

This is not to say that self-acceptance around dyslexia is always easy. I still meet the occasional person who will judge me negatively because of my condition. However, I've learned that the advantages that dyslexia has given me far outweigh the sting of those occasional negative perceptions.

## YOUR JOURNEY TO SELF-ACCEPTANCE

One more thing dyslexia has given me is a very deep understanding of the struggles that many other people have with different kinds of self-acceptance. This has been a powerful tool, as I've seen a very wide range of clients who are struggling with self-acceptance. Here are just a few examples:

- A woman who grew up in a poor family in the rural Appalachian region: She'd left home, worked her way through college and an MBA, and cultivated a corporate career. But she still often saw herself as that impoverished little girl, and she had a lot of shame about her background. At times of high stress, she'd question her "right" to be where she was. It was a classic case of "imposter syndrome." She lacked the self-acceptance to see how the resilience she'd gained from her background was the core of her success and value.

- A man who is a successful business leader but who also suffers from attention-deficit/hyperactivity disorder (ADHD): Like me with my dyslexia, he developed many coping strategies over the years that successfully got him through school and launched him into his career. However, he is still plagued by shame about his condition (he, too, keeps it a closely guarded secret) and a persistent fear that he might miss something in a business situation because he wasn't paying sufficient attention. He was unable to see that he has tremendous talent. It's the talent that has allowed him to compensate and to be so successful. Because he lacked sufficient self-acceptance (of both his ADHD and his innate talent), he feels unduly defined by his ADHD.

- A man who is a successful attorney, but who was also fired from his first job soon out of law school: The termination was conducted in an especially harsh and humiliating manner. He was in a tough situation, and he didn't do himself any favors, but the real issue was that he had landed with a tyrannical and abusive boss very early in his career. In the many years since, he's gotten back on track and has done very well for himself. But he's never gotten over that initial experience. He is always looking over his shoulder, is fearful, and comes off as an insecure leader. It's because he lacks the self-acceptance to move on from that early bad experience.

In these cases, as well as many others that I've seen, the path to self-acceptance includes five key steps:

1. **Let go of shame:** Shame is the key sign that there's something about ourselves that we're not accepting. In all the cases I've discussed, there was always some kind of personal shame at the root of the stories. Shame is a stagnant feeling because it doesn't allow for learning and growth, and the silence that usually accompanies shame leads to *paralysis*. But when we're aware of any shame we may be carrying, it can point to opportunities to work on our *Journey to Self-Acceptance.*

2. **Challenge self-imposed limitations:** One of the reasons shame can become so paralyzing is that it leads

FIGURE 22

THE JOURNEY TO SELF ACCEPTANCE

to self-imposed limitations. That was the case with my belief that dyslexia made me incapable of being a good writer or enjoying writing. One of the most effective ways out of the *paralysis* that shame can trigger is to challenge the shame-induced, self-imposed limitations. That often means attempting the things we're afraid we can't do and that we may even be embarrassed to try.

3. **Challenge the story you tell yourself or that others tell you:** Often, the self-imposed limitation is nothing more than a story that we've created or that we've told our-selves so many times that it has become a reality. "I have dyslexia, I can't spell or proofread well, so that means I can't be a writer" is nothing more than a story I'd cre-ated. Sometimes, the story that creates the self-limitation is one that others have created for us and that we've accepted for ourselves. In the case of the attorney who'd once been fired, he'd internalized a story his first boss had created about him, and that had destroyed his confidence.

The way forward was to use the success he'd subsequently built for himself to challenge the destructive story, create a more accurate picture of himself, and thus better accept and value himself.

4. **Be open to support when necessary:** One of the biggest impediments I've faced with dyslexia has not been the condition itself but rather my reluctance to accept support; this would have allowed me to better compensate for the condition and to better leverage my full abilities. For example, the fact that I didn't try to access extra support when I was in school (like more time for exams) and the secrecy I maintained around my dyslexia in my early career. That reluctance was again rooted in shame. Sometimes people with conditions like ADHD resist taking medication for the condition because of stigma. Elyn Saks, a renowned professor of both psychology and law at the University of Southern California, and also a person with schizophrenia, has written about her early-life reluctance to take the psychiatric medications she needs. Initially she viewed psychiatric medication as a "crutch," but later came to realize that getting past the stigma of taking medication was critical to her long-term success (Saks, 2007). One of the most important reasons to let go of shame is because shame discourages us from accepting the support we may need, and prevents us from reaching our full potential.

5. **Learn to see (and value) the strength on the other side of the limitation:** When we let go of shame, challenge self-imposed limitations, rewrite any negative stories that we create (or others create for us), and become open to receiving support, it opens the door to a completely

different view of what we perceive of as our limitations. Sometimes they turn into strengths. In my case, once I took these steps with respect to dyslexia, I became more aware of the unique strengths that the condition has also brought to my life. Today, there are parts of my dyslexia that I value, and I believe my dyslexia has also been a driving factor in much of my success.

## CHAPTER SUMMARY—PUTTING IT ALL TOGETHER

In this chapter, we discussed the last dimension of *The Thriving Mindset*: *The Journey to Self-Acceptance*.

### Some Key Points to Remember

- When people don't accept themselves (and fully value themselves), the lack of acceptance becomes a kind of headwind that can hold them back—preventing them from taking *Courageous Leaps* into their full potential.
- Self-acceptance sounds simple, but it's not. And a lack of self-acceptance is often a direct path into the *Adversity-Fear-Paralysis Cycle*.
- Most people struggle with self-acceptance at some point, and it can be especially challenging for people from an underprivileged or marginalized group—racialized minorities, members of the LGBTQ community, women, people with disabilities, etc.
- A major problem with the lack of self-acceptance is that it can lead to self-imposed limitations and other negative

self-talk. That's the source of the headwind that prevents *Courageous Leaps.*

- There are five major steps on *The Journey to Self-Acceptance:*
    1. Let go of shame
    2. Challenge self-imposed limitations
    3. Challenge any negative stories you tell yourself or that others tell you
    4. Be open to support when necessary
    5. Learn to see (and value) the strength on the other side of the limitation

## Key Questions to Think About:

1. Where are the areas where you haven't fully accepted (and valued) yourself? *(Hint: Most people have at least one.)*
2. What negative story might you be telling yourself about something that happened in your past?
3. Is there a negative story that someone else told you and that you've continued to carry forward and repeat?
4. What self-imposed limitations are you carrying?

# CONCLUSION

## THE MOST EXCITING TIME IN HUMAN HISTORY

At the beginning of this book, I referred to the era we're currently living through as the most disruptive time in human history. That's true, but there's another equally valid perspective: It's also the most exciting time in human history. That's because, when we understand the disruptive forces at play, and are thus able to leverage them appropriately, there is an opportunity and advantage to be found within the adversity of disruption. We can think of the disruption and excitement as opposite sides of the same coin.

Here's an example, and it's an extension of the story I told earlier about my struggles with dyslexia. In the early part of my life, dyslexia meant that I struggled with slow reading speed, which was a significant impediment to keeping pace with my peers. Today, that's changed. I can easily get through reading material as fast as my non-dyslexic professional colleagues, and sometimes significantly faster. That's because of a major disruption in the publishing industry: the advent of audiobooks and eBooks. In the past, I'd purchase a hardcopy book and secretly struggle to get through the material. Now, I purchase the audio version of the book, along with the eBook. I've discovered that I'm able to listen to audiobooks at very high speeds—typically between two-and-a-half and three times the normal speed, depending on the narrator's voice and diction. I then use the eBook version as a reference for anything I might want to review later. eBooks also have a word search feature that allows me to easily find specific sections by searching for a phrase.

Most of the people I've talked to about my "reading process" are amazed that I'm able to listen to and absorb material that fast. I suspect it may be because dyslexia has caused me to develop the skills of listening very intently and carefully. I still read short-form material (i.e., articles, case studies, etc.) the conventional way, but full books are now almost always a combination of the audiobook and eBook.

In my case, a disruptive change (i.e., the introduction of audiobooks and eBooks) has broken down a barrier and opened opportunities that were previously unavailable. It has enabled me to become an avid reader, something I've always wanted to be, but that had previously eluded me. Now, I always have a book close at hand. I sail through them, and I love it!

## THE EXCITEMENT ON THE OTHER SIDE OF DISRUPTION

My experience is not unique. There are many opportunities emerging as part of the rapid change of today's disruptive world. It's just a matter of being able to see and leverage the opportunity. Here are just a few examples:

- The pace of change and disruption in organizations means that the career stability our parents had (when people could spend an entire career advancing at a single company) is a thing of the past. However, this also means that we are no longer shackled to a single employer. There are also more and more flexible career opportunities available than ever before—if you've prepared yourself to access them.

- The pace of change means an ever decreasing need for manual labor and routine work, and people will need to constantly re-skill in order to remain productive and valuable. But that means creativity, critical thinking, and innovation are more valuable than ever, and ideas are the new currency. The key is to make yourself a life-long learner (and cultivate your *Intellectual Capital*) so that you have the idea-currency to be valuable.

- The shrinking world that interconnectivity and globalization have brought means that there's more competition than ever before. Geography is no longer a barrier. The Internet makes it possible for goods and services to be provided from virtually anywhere in the world. People and companies find themselves competing in a global marketplace like never before. But more interconnectivity also means more opportunity for people who live in far-flung and rural communities in the United States. They, too, can now participate in the global economy, provided they've done the preparation to make themselves competitive.

- As we've discussed in prior chapters, barriers to entry in many industries are continuing to drop. That has further destabilized many large companies and is accelerating turnover on the Fortune 100 list. However, because those barriers to entry are disappearing, there's now an enormous opportunity to be one of those new, disruptive market entrants.

In short, there's never been a better time to bring creative, original thinking forward. The key is to unlock your thinking so that you can participate in the emerging opportunities and become one of the people who benefits from the disruption.

## PARTICIPATING IN THE MOST EXCITING TIME IN HUMAN HISTORY

Cultivating a *Thriving Mindset* is the way to access emerging opportunities and thus participate in the most exciting time in human history. That requires three things, all of which we have outlined in this book. It requires an understanding of the new era (the *Learning Economy*) we now live in, an understanding of the *Adversity-Fear-Paralysis Cycle*, and an understanding of how to make the *Courageous Leaps* that lead to new opportunities. Making a *Courageous Leap* is not a simple, one-time process. A *Courageous Leap* is usually a long-term activity (one that can include setbacks and failures) that requires the *Power of Persistence* in order to achieve success.

## GOING FORWARD FROM HERE

With this book, you have the tools to prepare yourself for the opportunities that are unfolding—tools to help you create a path that is ideal for you. These tools can enable you to think creatively and innovatively, to engage in appropriate kinds of self-care, and find the *Self-Acceptance* that is critical for ***The Thriving Mindset.*** You now have the tools to build the *Intellectual Capital*, *Social Capital*, and *Financial Health* needed to succeed.

I invite you to leverage this book as a reference, to return to over time when you feel the storms of adversity and uncertainty arrive.

Thank you for reading!

# APPENDIX

# THE THRIVING MINDSET ASSESSMENT

(**Note:** You can also download an interactive and printable copy of the Thriving Mindset Assessment at the website: *MyThrivingMindset.com*)

## THRIVING MINDSET **ASSESSMENT**

**INSTRUCTIONS:**

Read each statement. Consider how true the statement is for you, and rate yourself on a scale of 1 to 5.

*Don't overthink.* There are 45 statements, but this assessment should be done rapidly. Your first instinct is most likely the right answer.

*Honesty provides the most value.* It's critical to be completely honest with yourself in this exercise. Remember, no one will see the answers except you, so focus on being as candid as you can.

1 = Not at all true for me
2 = Not very true for me
3 = Somewhat true for me
4 = Generally true for me
5 = Very true for me

1. When I set a goal, I see it through to the end.

2. I have a very clear idea of what I want to accomplish in the next 5 to 10 years.

3. I'm a very creative thinker.

4. I take great care of myself.

5. When I fall short of a goal, I'm great at getting over it and moving on.

6. I have an excellent handle on my personal/family finances.

7. I've read six or more books in the last year.

8. I have a supportive circle of friends and we keep in touch frequently.

9. I'm comfortable talking to others about my weaknesses.

10. I deliver on my promises, no matter what it takes.

11. I have a very clear understanding of my priorities in life.

12. I love taking on new and unfamiliar projects.

13. I always eat right.

14. I'm good at learning from my failures.

15. I (my family and I) have enough emergency savings to cover a year of living expenses.

16. I invest time every week in life-long learning and personal development.

17. I regularly attend networking events and professional conferences.

18. I am very good at listening to feedback, even if it's strong criticism.

19. I'm tenacious.

20. I know what I want to accomplish in my career.

21. I always find change and new challenges exciting.

22. I always get enough sleep.

23. It's okay if I fail at something, as long as I learned a lesson along the way.

24. I have a personal financial plan that is aligned with my goals & I update it at least once a year.

25. I have an excellent education.

26. I'm very good at following up with people I meet professionally, and I keep in touch with them.

27. I'm very proud of myself and of what I've accomplished.

28. I have a lot of self-discipline.

29. My work enables me to accomplish what's most important to me in life.

30. People I work with would describe me as innovative.

31. I get regular physicals and dental check-ups, and I follow my doctor's advice.

32. I never engage in self-criticism or negative self-talk.

33. I have a healthy relationship with money.

34. My education and professional training have made me extremely marketable.

35. I regularly act as a resource for people in my network and help them out when needed.

36. I'm very good at forgiving myself when I make a mistake.

37. When something becomes hard, I become even more committed to getting it done.

38. My work is very aligned with my personal values.

39. I'm naturally very curious and inquisitive.

40. I exercise at least five times a week.

41. I'm completely comfortable talking about my past failures.

42. I have a budget for my personal finances, and I always stick to it.

43. My friends and professional colleagues consider me extremely knowledgeable.

44. I always make meeting new people and getting to know them a very high priority.

45. There's nothing about me or my life that I'm ashamed of.

## NICE WORK! Let's Tally Your Score

Calculate your scores by copying your answer for each statement to the grid below. Add up your score across each row and write the sum in the TOTAL column on the right. *Remember, you can get an interactive version of this assessment that automatically tallies your scores at MyThrivingMindset.com.*

**YOUR SCORES:**

| chapter: | add statements: | | | | | TOTAL |
|---|---|---|---|---|---|---|
| 4. The Power of Persistence | #1 ___ + #10 ___ + #19 ___ + #28 ___ + #37 ___ = | | | | | |
| 5. Creating Your Path | #2 ___ + #11 ___ + #20 ___ + #29 ___ + #38 ___ = | | | | | |
| 6. Thinking Outside the Box | #3 ___ + #12 ___ + #21 ___ + #30 ___ + #39 ___ = | | | | | |
| 7. A Practice of Self-Care | #4 ___ + #13 ___ + #22 ___ + #31 ___ + #40 ___ = | | | | | |
| 8. Thriving Through Failure | #5 ___ + #14 ___ + #23 ___ + #32 ___ + #41 ___ = | | | | | |
| 9. Financial Health | #6 ___ + #15 ___ + #24 ___ + #33 ___ + #42 ___ = | | | | | |
| 10. Intellectual Captial | #7 ___ + #16 ___ + #25 ___ + #34 ___ + #43 ___ = | | | | | |
| 11. Social Capital | #8 ___ + #17 ___ + #26 ___ + #35 ___ + #44 ___ = | | | | | |
| 12. Self-Acceptance | #9 ___ + #18 ___ + #27 ___ + #36 ___ + #45 ___ = | | | | | |

These totals indicate your current proficiency in the **Dimensions of Thriving** from each chapter of the book.

A numerical score above 15 suggests that you're fairly proficient, while a score below 15 suggests this is an area of opportunity that you might want to give more attention.

*And remember, your score is just a starting point for you. The techniques provided in the book will allow you to quickly improve your proficiency in any area.*

| | |
|---|---|
| 21-25: | thriving |
| 16-20: | proficient |
| 6-15: | could improve |
| 0-5: | critical area of focus |

# ABOUT THE AUTHOR

**Gerry Valentine** inspires people to build resilience—to overcome setbacks, to look at challenges in new ways, and to turn adversity into a source of advantage. Gerry is a public speaker, executive coach, and business advisor with more than 25 years of experience as a Fortune 100 leader. As the founder of Vision Executive Coaching, he is a trusted advisor to corporate executives, business leaders, and entrepreneurs. Gerry specializes in teaching them how to use setbacks as a teacher; how to unlock creativity, imagination, and innovation; and how to use the best within oneself to inspire the very best in others.

Gerry built a career with some of the world's most respected firms, including American Express and Pfizer, where he led multi-million-dollar lines of business. But this was an unlikely path. Gerry's early life was spent in poverty, as the child of a single mother in a low-income part of New York City. He went on to earn a BS in Engineering from Cornell University and an MBA from the New York University Stern School of Management. Along the way, Gerry found that the adversity of his youth helped him develop the resilience he needed to succeed in the corporate world and that building resilience is a skill he can teach others.

Today, Gerry gives keynote talks and workshops across the country on building resilience, leading during difficult times, and finding strategic solutions to challenges. He is a TEDx speaker and a contributor to Forbes.com. Gerry has also lectured on executive leadership at Columbia University, Baruch College, and Colorado State University.

Gerry divides his time between New York City and New Paltz, New York—a picturesque town on the Hudson River Valley. He's an outdoor enthusiast who enjoys running, cycling, hiking, and skiing. Gerry has also completed eight Ironman Triathlons, five marathons, and many shorter-distance events.

## CONTACT INFORMATION:

Email:     Gerry@GerryValentine.com
LinkedIn:  https://www.linkedin.com/in/gerryvalentine
Twitter:   https://twitter.com/gerryval
Website:   www.GerryValentine.com

# BIBLIOGRAPHY

Alltucker, Ken. 2019. *'Really Astonishing': Average Cost of Hospital ER Visit Surges 176% in a Decade, Report Says.* June 4. Accessed August 16, 2020. https://www. usatoday.com/story/news/health/2019/06/04/hospital-billing-code-changes-help-explain-176-surge-er-costs/1336321001/.

Amazon Staff. n.d. *What Robots Do (and don't do) at Amazon Fulfillment Centers.* Accessed August 12, 2020. https://www.aboutamazon.com/amazon-fulfillment/our-innovation/what-robots-do-and-dont-do-at-amazon-fulfillment-centers/.

Backman, Maurie. 2017. *16.6 Million U.S. Households Have a Negative Net Worth – Here's the Surprising Reason Why.* May 14. Accessed August 16, 2020. https://www.fool.com/retirement/2017/05/14/166-million-us-households-have-a-negative-net-wort.aspx.

Bahney, Anna. 2019. *College Grads Earn $30,000 a Year More Than People with Just a High School Degree.* June 6. Accessed August 12, 2020. https://www.cnn.com/2019/06/06/success/college-worth-it/index.html.

Bastrikin, Andrej. 2020. *Student Loan Debt Statistics.* April 12. Accessed August 16, 2020. https://education data.org/student-loan-debt-statistics/.

Belgrave, Danielle, and Anja Thieme. 2019. *Microsoft Research Blog.* October 2. Accessed August 13, 2020. https://www.microsoft.com/en-us/research/blog/ microsoft-collaborates-with-silvercloud-health-to- develop-ai-for-improved-mental-health/.

Boland, Brodie, Aaron De Smet, Rob Palter, and Aditya Sanghvi. 2020. *Reimagining The Office and Work Life After COVID-19.* June 8. Accessed August 20, 2020. https://www.mckinsey.com/business-functions/organization/ our-insights/reimagining-the-office-and-work-life-after- covid-19.

Bonnet, Didier, Jerome Buvat, and Subrahmanyam KVJ. n.d. *When Digital Disruption Strikes: How Can Incumbents Respond?* Accessed 2020 12, August. https://www. capgemini.com/consulting/wp-content/uploads/ sites/30/2017/07/digital_disruption_1.pdf.

Borrell, Luisa N., Lisa Graham, and Sharon P. Joseph. 2016. *Associations of Neighborhood Safety and Neighborhood Support with Overweight and Obesity in US Children and Adolescents.* October 20. Accessed August 13, 2020. https:// www.ncbi.nlm.nih.gov/pmc/articles/PMC5072475/.

Bowers, Brent. 2007. "Study Shows Stronger Links Between Entrepreneurs and Dyslexia." *The New York Times.* November 5. Accessed August 16, 2020. https://www. nytimes.com/2007/12/05/business/worldbusiness/05iht- dyslexia.4.8602036.html.

Bradger, Emily. 2018. *Extensive Data Shows Punishing Reach of Racism for Black Boys.* March 19. Accessed August 12, 2020. https://www.nytimes.com/interactive/2018/03/19/upshot/race-class-white-and-black-men.html.

Bughin, Jacques, Eric Hazan, Susan Lund, Peter Dahlström, Anna Wiesinger, and Amresh Subramaniam. 2018. *"Skill shift: Automation and the future of the workforce." McKinsey & Company.* May 23. Accessed August 12, 2020. https://www.mckinsey.com/featured-insights/future-of-work/skill-shift-automation-and-the-future-of-the-workforce.

Burner, Trent, Liz Supinski, Susan Zhu, Samuel Robinson, and Cate Supinski. 2019. "The Skills Gap 2019." *Society for Human Resource Management (SHRM).* Accessed August 16, 2020. https://www.shrm.org/hr-today/trends-and-forecasting/research-and-surveys/Pages/Skills-Gap-2019.aspx.

Bustamante, Jaleesa. 2019. *Average Cost of College & Tuition.* June 7. Accessed August 16, 2020. https://educationdata.org/average-cost-of-college/.

Carlson, Nicholas. 2010. *At last—The Full Story of How Facebook Was Founded.* May 5. Accessed August 16, 2020. https://www.businessinsider.com/how-facebook-was-founded-2010-3.

Carnevale, Anthony P., Stephen J. Rose, and Ban Cheah. 2011. *The College Payoff – Education, Occupations, Life Earnings.* Accessed August 16, 2020. https://cew.georgetown.edu/wp-content/uploads/collegepayoff-completed.pdf.

Center for Disease Control & Prevention. n.d. *National Center for Health Statistics*. Accessed August 17, 2020. https://www.cdc.gov/nchs/fastats/life-expectancy.htm.

Center for Disease Control. 2019. *Prevalence of Childhood Obesity in the United States*. June 24. Accessed August 13, 2020. https://www.cdc.gov/obesity/data/childhood.html.

Cherry, Kendra. 2019. *"How You Can Tell That You're an Introvert." Very Well Mind*. October 18. Accessed August 16, 2020. https://www.verywellmind.com/signs-you-are-an-introvert-2795427#:~:text=While%20introverts%20make%20up%20an,misconceptions%20about%20this%20personality%20type.

Chetty, Raj, Maggie R. Jones, and Sonya R. Porter. 2018. *Race and Economic Opportunity in the United States: An Intergenerational Perspective*. March. Accessed August 12, 2020. http://www.equality-of-opportunity.org/assets/documents/race_paper.pdf.

Chui, Michael, James Manyika, and Mehdi Miremadi. 2015. *Four Fundamentals of Workplace Automation*. November 1. Accessed August 16, 2020. https://www.mckinsey.com/business-functions/mckinsey-digital/our-insights/four-fundamentals-of-workplace-automation.

Clement, J. 2020. *Global Digital Population as of July 2020*. July 24. Accessed August 13, 2020. https://www.statista.com/statistics/617136/digital-population-worldwide/.

——. 2020. *Number of Global Social Network Users 2017–2025*. July 15. Accessed August 12, 2020. https://www.statista.com/statistics/278414/number-of-worldwide-social-network-users/#:~:text=Social%20media%20usage%20is%20one,almost%204.41%20 billion%20in%202025.&text=Social%20network%20 penetration%20is%20constantly,2020%20stood%20 at%2049%20percent.

Del Rey, Jason. 2019. *How Robots are Transforming Amazon Warehouse Jobs—for better and worse.* December 11. Accessed August 12, 2020. https://www. vox.com/recode/2019/12/11/20982652/robots-amazon-warehouse-jobs-automation.

Deming, David. 2019. *In the Salary Race, Engineers Sprint but English Majors Endure.* October 1. Accessed August 16, 2020. https://www.nytimes.com/2019/09/20/business/liberal-arts-stem-salaries.html.

DeSilver, Drew. 2017. *Most Americans Unaware That as U.S. Manufacturing Jobs Have Disappeared, Output Has Grown.* July 25. Accessed August 18, 2020. https:// www.pewresearch.org/fact-tank/2017/07/25/most-americans-unaware-that-as-u-s-manufacturing-jobs-have-disappeared-output-has-grown/.

Detrixhe, John. 2019. "It Took 43 of The World's Fastest Runners to Break The 2-Hour Marathon Barrier." *Quartz.* October 13. Accessed August 16, 2020. https:// qz.com/1727150/breaking-marathon-barrier-required-43-world-class-runners/.

Domonoske, Camila. 2020. *An Electric Pickup Truck Brings New Energy To Lordstown, Ohio.* June 23. Accessed August 13, 2020. https://www.npr.org/2020/06/23/88094 1975/an-electric-pickup-truck-brings-new-energy-to-lordstown-ohio.

Drucker, Peter. 2016. *The Effective Executive: The Definitive Guide to Getting the Right Things Done.* New York: HarperCollins Publishers.

Estrin, James. 2015. *Kodak's First Digital Moment.* August 12. Accessed August 13, 2020. https://lens.blogs. nytimes.com/2015/08/12/kodaks-first-digital-moment/.

FINR Investor Education Foundation. 2018. *National Financial Capability Study.* October. Accessed August 16, 2020. https://www.usfinancialcapability.org/results.php? region=US.

Friedman, Zack. 2019. *78% Of Workers Live Paycheck To Paycheck.* January 11. Accessed August 16, 2020. https://www.forbes.com/sites/zackfriedman/2019/01/11/ live-paycheck-to-paycheck-government-shutdown/ #453a02e74f10.

Funding Universe. n.d. *Columbia House Company History.* Accessed August 16, 2020. http://www.fundinguniverse. com/company-histories/columbia-house-company-history/.

Gabler, Neal. 2016. *The Secret Shame of Middle-Class Americans.* May. Accessed August 13, 2020. https:// www.theatlantic.com/magazine/archive/2016/05/my-secret-shame/476415/.

Gibney, Elizabeth. 2019. *Hello Quantum World! Google Publishes Landmark Quantum Supremacy Claim.* October 23. Accessed August 13, 202. https://www. nature.com/articles/d41586-019-03213-z.

Grady, Denise. 2019. *A.I. Took a Test to Detect Lung Cancer. It Got an A.* May 20. Accessed August 12, 2020. https://www.nytimes.com/2019/05/20/health/cancer-artificial-intelligence-ct-scans.html#:~:text=Artificial%20 intelligence%20may%20help%20doctors,to%20 screen%20for%20lung%20cancer.&text=Computers%20

were%20as%20good%20or,Google%20and%20 several%20medical%20ce.

Grieco, Elizabeth. 2020. *U.S. newspapers have shed half of their newsroom employees since 2008.* August 12. Accessed August 12, 2020. https://www.pewresearch. org/fact-tank/2020/04/20/u-s-newsroom-employment-has-dropped-by-a-quarter-since-2008/.

Griswold, Alison, and Dylan Love. 2013. "17 Business Titans Who Overcame Dyslexia." *Business Insider.* October 25. Accessed August 16, 2020. https://www.businessinsider. com/business-titans-who-overcame-dyslexia-2013-10.

Gross, Daniel A. 2019. *How Elite US schools Give Preference to Wealthy and White 'Legacy' Applicants.* January 23. Accessed August 13, 2020. https://www.theguardian. com/us-news/2019/jan/23/elite-schools-ivy-league-legacy-admissions-harvard-wealthier-whiter.

Hackett, Conard, and David McClendon. 2017. *Christians Remain World's Largest Religious Group, But They are Declining in Europe.* April 5. Accessed August 12, 2020. https://www.pewresearch.org/fact-tank/2017/04/05/ christians-remain-worlds-largest-religious-group-but-they-are-declining-in-europe/.

Hassan, Adeel. 2019. *Hate-Crime Violence Hits 16-Year High, F.B.I. Reports.* November 12. Accessed August 13, 2020. https://www.nytimes.com/2019/11/12/us/hate-crimes-fbi-report.html.

Hicks, Michael J., and Srikant Devaraj. 2015. "The Myth and Reality of Manufacturing in America." *Ball State University Center for Economic Research.* June. Accessed August 17, 2020. https://projects.cberdata.org/reports/MfgReality.pdf.

Jones, Matt. 2018. *How to Deal With Your Car's Negative Equity.* April 6. Accessed August 16, 2020. https://www.edmunds.com/car-buying/being-upside-down.html.

Kalfman, Dan. n.d. *The End of the Line.* Accessed August 13, 2020. https://www.nytimes.com/interactive/2019/05/01/magazine/lordstown-general-motors-plant.html.

Keh, Andrew. 2019. "Eliud Kipchoge Breaks Two-Hour Marathon Barrier." *The New York Times.* October 14. Accessed August 16, 2020. https://www.nytimes.com/2019/10/12/sports/eliud-kipchoge-marathon-record.html.

Khalil, Ashraf, Amy Jeff, and Carolyn Thompson. 2019. *American Students' Performance Lags on Nation's Report Card.* October 30. Accessed August 13, 202. https://apnews.com/565be54d26354e72b02a813593923fef.

Kichhar, Rakesh. 2020. *Unemployment Rose Higher in Three Months of COVID-19 Than it Did in Two Years of the Great Recession.* June 11. Accessed August 18, 2020. https://www.pewresearch.org/fact-tank/2020/06/11/unemployment-rose-higher-in-three-months-of-covid-19-than-it-did-in-two-years-of-the-great-recession/.

Koetsier, John. 2020. *6 Reasons Most Want To Work From Home Even After Coronavirus.* June 13. Accessed August 20, 2020. https://www.forbes.com/sites/johnkoetsier/2020/06/13/6-reasons-most-want-to-work-from-home-even-after-coronavirus/#4f70174938fa.

Lending Club & Harris Poll. 2018. *Is Your Financial Health Affecting Your Quality of Life?* August 20. Accessed August 16, 2020. https://www.lendingclub.com/research/financial-health?utm_medium=press_release&utm_

source=pr_newswire&utm_campaign=pl_financial_health_2018_q4.

Lua, Alfred. n.d. *21 Top Social Media Sites to Consider for Your Brand*. Accessed August 12, 2020. https://buffer.com/library/social-media-sites/.

Maldonado, Camilo. 2018. *Price Of College Increasing Almost 8 Times Faster Than Wages*. July 24. Accessed August 16, 2020. https://www.forbes.com/sites/camilomaldonado/2018/07/24/price-of-college-increasing-almost-8-times-faster-than-wages/#8290a6366c1d.

Manyika, James, Susan Lund, Michael Chui, Jacques Bughin, Jonathan Woetzel, Parul Batra, Ryan Ko, and Saurabh Sanghvi. 2017. *Jobs Lost, Jobs Gained: What the future of work will mean for jobs, skills, and wages*. November 28. Accessed August 13, 2020. https://www.mckinsey.com/featured-insights/future-of-work/jobs-lost-jobs-gained-what-the-future-of-work-will-mean-for-jobs-skills-and-wages.

Marr, Bernard. 2020. *Demand For These Autonomous Delivery Robots Is Skyrocketing During This Pandemic*. May 29. Accessed August 20, 2020. https://www.forbes.com/sites/bernardmarr/2020/05/29/demand-for-these-autonomous-delivery-robots-is-skyrocketing-during-this-pandemic/#7a2871927f3c.

McCraken, Harry. 2018. *Google CEO: AI is a Bigger Deal Than Fire or Electricity*. January 19. Accessed August 13, 2020. https://www.fastcompany.com/40519204/google-sundar-pichai-ai-is-a-bigger-deal-than-fire-or-electricity.

McDermid, Riley. 2017. *Airbnb's Number of Listings Surpasses Rooms Held by Top 5 Hotel Brands Combined.*

April 11. Accessed August 12, 2020. https://www.
bizjournals.com/sanfrancisco/news/2017/08/11/airbnb-
surpasses-ihg-wyn-hilton-marriott-listings.html.

——. 2017. *San Francisco Business Times*. April 11.
Accessed August 12, 2020. https://www.bizjournals.com/
sanfrancisco/news/2017/08/11/airbnb-surpasses-ihg-
wyn-hilton-marriott-listings.html.

Merriam-Webster. 2020. *Merriam-Webster Dictionary
– Crucible*. Accessed August 17, 2020. https://www.
merriam-webster.com/dictionary/crucible.

Moyers & Company. 2014. *Neil deGrasse Tyson on Science
Literacy*. January 24. Accessed August 16, 2020. https://
billmoyers.com/episode/neil-degrasse-tyson-on-science-
literacy/.

Muro, Mark, Jacob Winton, and Robert Maxim. 2019. *WHAT
JOBS ARE AFFECTED BY AI? Better-paid, better-educated
workers face the most exposure*. November. Accessed
August 12, 2020. https://www.brookings.edu/wp-content/
uploads/2019/11/2019.11.20_BrookingsMetro_What-
jobs-are-affected-by-AI_Report_Muro-Whiton-
Maxim.pdf#page=11.

National Center for Education Statistics. n.d. *College
Navigator – Harvard University*. Accessed August 16,
2020. https://nces.ed.gov/collegenavigator/?id=166027.

Nobel Prize Foundation. n.d. *Malala Yousafzai Biographical*.
Accessed August 13, 2020. https://www.nobelprize.org/
prizes/peace/2014/yousafzai/biographical/.

Oxford Economics. 2019. "How Robots Will Change the
World - What Automation Really Means for Productivity."
*Oxford Economics*. June. Accessed August 17, 2020.

https://www.oxfordeconomics.com/recent-releases/
how-robots-change-the-world.

Parker, Kim. 2012. *Yes, the Rich Are Different.* August 27. Accessed August 16, 2020. https://www.pewsocialtrends. org/2012/08/27/yes-the-rich-are-different/.

Porter, Jon. 2019. *Boston Dynamics' Atlas Can Now Do an Impressive Gymnastics Routine.* September 4. Accessed August 13, 2020. https://www.theverge.com/ 2019/9/24/20881385/boston-dynamics-atlas-gymnastics-routine-somersaults-split-leap.

Reed, Phil. 2020. *Anxiety and Social Media Use.* February 3. Accessed August 16, 2020. https://www.psychologytoday. com/us/blog/digital-world-real-world/202002/ anxiety-and-social-media-use.

Reeves, Richard V., and Eleanor Krause. 2018. *Raj Chetty in 14 Charts: Big findings on opportunity and mobility we should all know.* January 11. Accessed August 16, 2020. https://www.brookings.edu/blog/social-mobility-memos/ 2018/01/11/raj-chetty-in-14-charts-big-findings-on-opportunity-and-mobility-we-should-know/.

Roser, Max, Esteban Ortiz-Ospina, and Hannah Ritchie. 2019. *Life Expectancy.* October. Accessed August 13, 2020. https://ourworldindata.org/life-expectancy.

Saks, Elyn. 2007. *The Center Cannot Hold: My Journey Through Madness.* New York: Hachette Books.

Sawhill, Isabel V., and Edward Rodrigue. 2015. *Wealth, Inheritance, and Social Mobility.* January 15. Accessed August 16, 2020. https://www.brookings.edu/blog/social-mobility-memos/2015/01/30/wealth-inheritance-and-social-mobility/.

Schwab, Klaus. n.d. *The Fourth Industrial Revolution.* Accessed August 13, 2020. https://www.weforum.org/pages/the-fourth-industrial-revolution-by-klaus-schwab.

Segran, Elizabeth. 2018. *How a Warehouse Fire Sparked Company-wide Innovation at Gap Inc.* July 31. Accessed August 16, 2020. https://www.fastcompany.com/90205911/how-a-warehouse-fire-at-gap-sparked-company-wide-innovation.

Sneader, Kevin, and Shubham Singhal. 2020. *Beyond Coronavirus: The path to the next normal.* March 23. Accessed August 20, 2020. https://www.mckinsey.com/industries/healthcare-systems-and-services/our-insights/beyond-coronavirus-the-path-to-the-next-normal.

Steadman, Ian. 2013. *IBM's Watson is Better at Diagnosing Cancer Than Human Doctors.* February 11. Accessed August 13, 2020. https://www.wired.co.uk/article/ibm-watson-medical-doctor.

Steverman, Ben. 2019. *The Wealth Detective Who Finds the Hidden Money of the Super Rich.* May 23. Accessed August 16, 2020. https://www.bloomberg.com/news/features/2019-05-23/the-wealth-detective-who-finds-the-hidden-money-of-the-super-rich?srnd=premium.

Strochic, Nina. 2020. *U.S. Coronavirus Deaths Now Surpass Fatalities in the Vietnam War.* April 28. Accessed August 20, 2020. https://www.nationalgeographic.com/history/2020/04/coronavirus-death-toll-vietnam-war-cvd/#close.

Tami Luhby, Tami. 2016. *76 Million Americans are Struggling Financially or Just Getting By.* June 10. Accessed August 16, 2020. https://money.cnn.com/2016/06/10/news/economy/americans-struggling-financially/index.html.

Tate, Nick. 2018. *Loneliness Rivals Obesity, Smoking as Health Risk*. May 4. Accessed August 16, 2020. https://www.webmd.com/balance/news/20180504/loneliness-rivals-obesity-smoking-as-health-risk.

Tavernise, Sabrina. 2019. *With His Job Gone, An Autoworker Wonders, 'What Am I as a Man?'* May 27. Accessed August 13, 2020. https://www.nytimes.com/2019/05/27/us/auto-worker-jobs-lost.html?smid=pc-thedaily.

The Ascent. 2018. *Here's the Average American's Credit Card Debt – and How to Get Yours Under Control.* November 20. Accessed August 16, 2020. https://www.fool.com/the-ascent/credit-cards/articles/heres-the-average-americans-credit-card-debt-and-h/.

The Encyclopaedia Britannica. n.d. *Industrial Revolution.* Accessed August 13, 2020. https://www.britannica.com/event/Industrial-Revolution#ref3504.

The Federal Reserve. 2017. *Federal Reserve Board Issues Report on the Economic Well-Being of U.S. Households.* May 19. Accessed August 16, 2020. https://www.federalreserve.gov/newsevents/pressreleases/other20170519a.htm.

The International Dyslexia Association. n.d. "Dyslexia Basics." *The International Dyslexia Association.* Accessed August 16, 2020. https://dyslexiaida.org/dyslexia-basics.

The New York Times. 2020. *About 30 Million Workers Are Collecting Jobless Benefits.* July 24. Accessed August 18, 2020. https://www.nytimes.com/live/2020/07/23/business/stock-market-today-coronavirus.

———. 2020. *Coronavirus Map: Tracking the Global Outbreak.* August 18. Accessed August 18, 2020. https://www.nytimes.com/interactive/2020/world/coronavirus-maps.html.

——. 2020. *U.S. Added 1.8 Million Jobs in July.* August 10. Accessed August 18, 2020. https://www. nytimes.com/live/2020/08/07/business/stock-market-today-coronavirus.

Thompson, Derek. 2011. *Who's Had the Worst Recession: Boomers, Millennials, or Gen-Xers?* September 13. Accessed August 13, 2020. https://www.theatlantic.com/business/archive/2011/09/whos-had-the-worst-recession-boomers-millennials-or-gen-xers/245056/.

Urban, Peter. 2019. *Gen Xers Overlooked for Job Promotions.* July 29. Accessed August 13, 2020. https://www.aarp.org/work/working-at-50-plus/info-2019/gen-x-missing-job-promotions.html.

Valinsky, Jordan. 2020. *Business is booming for these 14 companies during the coronavirus pandemic.* July 2. Accessed August 20, 2020. https://www.cnn.com/2020/05/07/business/companies-thriving-coronavirus-pandemic/index.html.

Wattles, Jackie. 2015. *Columbia House Files for Bankruptcy.* August 10. Accessed August 16, 2020. https://money.cnn.com/2015/08/10/news/columbia-house-bankruptcy/index.html.

Web MD. 2020. *Viagra: How a Little Blue Pill Changed the World.* February 24. Accessed August 16, 2020. https://www.drugs.com/slideshow/viagra-little-blue-pill-1043#:~:text=The%20sildenafil%20compound%20was%20originally,inducing%20erections%20than%20treating%20angina.

Wilkerson, Isabel. 2011. *The Warmth of Other Suns THE EPIC STORY OF AMERICA'S GREAT MIGRATION.* Vol. 1. New York: Penguin Random House.

Wong, Alia. 2018. *Why Millions of Teens Can't Finish Their Homework.* October 30. Accessed August 16, 2020. https://www.theatlantic.com/education/archive/2018/10/lacking-Internet-millions-teens-cant-do-homework/574402/.

Wong, Kristin. 2018. *The 6 Steps to Turning Setbacks Into Advantages.* January 30. Accessed August 13, 2020. https://www.nytimes.com/2018/01/30/smarter-living/six-stages-of-setbacks-help-growth.html.

Zaloom, Caitlin. 2019. *STEM Is Overrated – College is not just job prep, and the job market changes constantly.* September 10. Accessed August 16, 2020. https://www.theatlantic.com/ideas/archive/2019/09/college-not-job-prep/597487/.

CPSIA information can be obtained
at www.ICGtesting.com
Printed in the USA
BVHW091340191221
624398BV00003B/3